LISTENING HEARTS:
DISCERNING CALL IN COMMUNITY

Listening

Morehouse Publishing
NEW YORK · HARRISBURG · DENVER

Suzanne G. Farnham
Joseph P. Gill
R. Taylor McLean
Susan M. Ward

Hearts

Discerning Call in Community

Newly Revised Edition
with a Foreword by Parker J. Palmer

Morehouse Publishing, 4775 Linglestown Road,
Harrisburg, PA 17112
Morehouse Publishing, 445 Fifth Avenue, New York, NY 10016
Morehouse Publishing is an imprint of Church Publishing Incorporated.
www.churchpublishing.org

Unless otherwise noted, the Scripture quotations contained herein
are from the New Revised Standard Version Bible, copyright © 1989
by the Division of Christian Education of the National Council of
Churches of Christ in the U.S.A. Used by permission.
All rights reserved.

Excerpt from *The Irrational Season* by Madeleine L'Engle.
Copyright © 1977 by Crosswicks, Ltd. Reprinted by permission
of HarperCollins Publishers.

Prayer adapted from *Thoughts in Solitude* by Thomas Merton.
Copyright © 1956, 1958 by the Abbey of Our Lady of
Gethsemani. Reprinted by permission of Farrar, Straus,
and Giroux, Inc.

Library of Congress Cataloging-in-Publication Data

Listening hearts : discerning call in community /
Suzanne G. Farnham... [et al.].
p. cm
Includes bibliographical references.

ISBN 13 : 978-0-8192-2444-6
1. Vocation. 2. Discernment of spirits. 3. Christian communities.
4. Spiritual life—Anglican authors. I. Farnham, Suzanne G.
BV1740.L57   1991
253—dc2091.2220
CIP

Printed in the United States of America

To JENIFER BALLARD RAMBERG, our friend and co-worker, who experienced her own personal struggle with hearing God's call. Her unique contributions came from her knowledge of feminist theology, and she guided and prodded us in the early stages of this book's development. Her untimely death is felt deeply by each of us individually, and our working group has sorely missed her.

Contents

Acknowledgments

As part of the Christian Vocation Project, four of us worked together in Christian community to write this book. We could not have done it without vast amounts of help from the larger Church community. Substantial support, including funding, came from Memorial Episcopal Church in Baltimore and from the Diocese of Maryland, where the project was a CROSS + ROADS Program.

Among the many people crucial to the endeavor, five highly qualified persons were consistently available upon request from the very beginning. Patricia Scanlan of the Baltimore Carmelite Sisters provided encouragement and guidance of incalculable value. Russell Ayers, director of the Life/Work Planning Center in Washington, D.C., offered continuing counsel and evaluation as consultant for the project. John McIntyre served as in-house copy editor with extraordinary competence. Chris Hotvedt, a freelance graphic designer in Baltimore, developed the logo and designed the book. The Reverend William Rich, chaplain of Goucher College, where he was a member of the department of philosophy and religion, provided important critical insights throughout.

An immense amount of research preceded the writing of this book, including extensive reading, interviews, and consultation. Nearly fifty people assisted: Patricia Ashby, the Reverend Andrew Barasda, Alma Bell, Kathleen Capcara, Barbara Cates, Barbara Chalmers, Anne Cromwell, the Reverend John Diehl, Sr. Elaine of the All Saints Sisters of the Poor, Jeffrey Eller, the Reverend Lyman Farnham, Pamela Fleming, Robert Hunt, Gregory Jones, Mary Keath, Jean Kennedy, Sr. Kathleen Kirk, O.C.D., the Reverend Canon John Kitagawa, Sherry Kolbe, Margie Lance, Mary Ann Lewis, Constance Lieder, Sally Maulsby, Kim McDonald, John McIntyre, Patricia McIntyre, Bruce McPherson, Louise Miller, Caroline Naylor, Jenifer Ramberg, Richard Roszel, Jeannine Ruof, Lois Schenck, Alwilda Scholler-Jaquish, Lynne Schon, Barbara Seras, Wendy Shuford, Keith Smith, Canon Rosemary Snapp, Cynthia Spencer, Jocelyn Traynham, Gayle Turner, the Reverend Mother Virginia of the All Saints Sisters of the Poor, Amelia Ward, and Peter Wilcock.

Others provided support services: Paul Beares, Marilynn Cornejo, Elizabeth Duvall, the Reverend Albert Halverstadt, Jr., Susan Walters, and Susan Weeks. This list does not include the many, many people who, apart from the book, helped with the Christian Vocation Project itself.

People with varied backgrounds commented on our work as the manuscript developed: Edith

Donahue, Sr. Rose Mary Dougherty, the Very
Reverend James Fenhagen, the Reverend Albert
Halverstadt, Jr., the Reverend Canon James Ransom,
Canon Sally Robinson, Dorothy Rosenthal, Andrew
Schenck, Lois Schenck, the Reverend David Scott,
the Reverend Michael Sheeran, S.J., Frank Shivers,
and Frances Young.

Still others supplied information, ideas, sugges-
tions, and encouragement: the Reverend Michelle
Bond, the Reverend Locke Bowman, the Reverend
Celine Burke, the Right Reverend John Coburn, the
Reverend John Docker, the Right Reverend Mark
Dyer, the Right Reverend A. Theodore Eastman,
the Reverend Tilden Edwards, the Reverend Gerald
Goethe, the Reverend Margaret Guenther, Jean
Haldane, Barbara Hanst, Sr. Rita Anne Houlihan,
R.C., Virginia Levering, Keith Man, the Reverend
Loren Mead, Parker Palmer, the Reverend Albert
Peters, Barbara Platt, the Right Reverend Alexander
Stewart, Nancy Tunnessen, and the Reverend John
Westerhoff.

Four diverse parishes served as field-test sites,
with many people providing suggestions that
refined and strengthened the material: Epiphany
Church, Odenton, Md.; the Church of the Holy
Comforter, Vienna, Va.; Memorial Episcopal
Church, Baltimore, Md.; and St. Mark's,
Boonsboro, Md.

Finally, we offered thanks for our four spouses who
unwittingly found themselves silent partners in this
enterprise: the Reverend F. Lyman Farnham, Sheila
McDonald Gill, Peggy M. McLean, and Sibley L.

Ward III. They were remarkably patient and support-ive through more than two years as we immersed ourselves in writing this book together.

Three additional people provided strong support as we prepared this Special 20th Anniversary Edition. Frances Sullinger gave invaluable help in revis-ing the appendices. Parker Palmer ever so kindly wrote a foreword for the book. And our new editor, the Reverend Stephanie Spellers, offered sensitive, insightful encouragement and guidance. We are grateful for all the people, twenty years ago and now, who gave graciously of their time to bring this work to fruition.

Foreword to 20th Anniversary Edition of Listening Hearts

I met Suzanne Farnham in April of 1987 at a retreat I co-led with Walter and June Wink at Kirkridge. I was grateful for the quality of her presence and participation, and I was glad to see her again at another conference in the early 1990s. I *thought* I remembered her well. But the accuracy of my memory was called into serious doubt when Suzanne spoke to the group and said, "Parker Palmer is the father of my child."

That part of our Kirkridge experience I did *not* remember. Nor do I remember what I said, if anything, after Suzanne's comment got everyone's attention, including mine. But I was relieved when she explained, amid much laughter, that her "child" was the 1991 book *Listening Hearts* (co-authored with Joseph Gill, R. Taylor McLean, and Susan Ward) which had been inspired, in part, by elements of the Kirkridge retreat.

For a twenty-year-old, this book has served so many people so well that I am proud to claim a very minor role in its lineage. I am also grateful for a chance to say a few words about it, because *Listening Hearts* focuses on a question that has been very close to my heart for a long time: How can we listen for our vocation, for God's calling in our lives, and listen for it in community, in the Body of Christ?

In my mid-thirties, at a time when my own calling was a source of great confusion to me, I was attracted to Quakerism. My attraction had much to do with the twin pillars of Quaker spirituality as I understand it: the conviction that every human being has direct inward access to God, and the equally strong conviction that we need a community of discernment to help us sort and sift what we *think* we are hearing from within. As depth psychology and good theology remind us—and as many of us know from experience—not every voice from within is the voice of God. It is easy to find examples of people who have mistaken the voice of ego or some deeper darkness for the voice of truth, following it down a path of personal ruination, sometimes taking others with them.

So listening for one's calling is tricky business. From personal experience I know that one's hearing can be blocked by a wide range of inner dynamics, from thinking too poorly of yourself to thinking too highly of yourself. If I suffer from ego inflation, I am likely to have grandiose visions of what I can do in the world, leading me into activities that will damage me or others. If I suffer from ego deflation, I am likely to shy away from an important calling that will stretch me but that I have the gifts to pursue.

In *Let Your Life Speak*, I tell about a moment when I felt sure that becoming the president of a small educational institution was the thing for me. I took my—well, my ego—to a Clearness Committee, a Quaker discernment process mentioned in *Listening Hearts*. About an hour into the process (after I had answered many questions about my calling with a certainty which had begun to feel not exactly God-given), someone asked me a simple question: "What would you like most about being president?"

I thought for a while, decided it was time to get honest, then started listing things I would *not* like. My list was long, ranging from how I would have to dress, to being on call all the time, to my intense dislike of faculty politics. My questioner gently reminded me that the question was about what I would *like*. I thought some more and—having tired of answering questions from my ego rather than my heart—I finally said, sheepishly, "I guess the only thing I'd really like is seeing my picture in the paper with the word 'president' under it."

After a studied silence in which I had to stew in my own answer, my questioner spoke again: "Parker, can you think of an easier way to get your picture in the paper?"

That story makes me laugh, of course, at myself. But it also evokes my gratitude. As a person who lacks some of the key gifts necessary for institutional leadership, the decision I made to turn down that presidency and keep seeking my true calling saved me—and the educational institution in question—from a sad fate. I am deeply grateful for the way a true community of discernment can help us sift and winnow the many messages we get from inside and outside of ourselves, separating the wheat from the chaff.

Creating and holding a space for discernment is profoundly counter-cultural work. We live in a culture that too often regards us as empty vessels to be filled with someone else's knowledge, someone else's agenda, someone else's truth—and churches can be among the worst offenders in this regard. Spiritual discernment is not about telling each other what to do. Spiritual discernment is about trusting the fact that all of us are made in God's image and all of us have access to God's call for our lives. It is about practicing the disciplines required to help ourselves and each other heal the internal wounds and surmount the external obstacles that keep us from hearing that call.

Listening Hearts is a book that has helped tens of thousands of people in the churches do exactly that. I cannot lay claim to being its proud father. But as a more distant relative, I commend this book to you, doing so with enthusiasm and gratitude as it enters its third decade of service.

Parker J. Palmer
Author of *A Hidden Wholeness,*
Let Your Life Speak, and
The Courage to Teach
October 2010

LISTENING HEARTS:
DISCERNING CALL IN COMMUNITY

Introduction

"Find a place in your heart," implores Theophan the Recluse, "and speak there with the Lord. It is the Lord's reception room."[1]

God loves each one of us, beckoning us into a relationship that is personal, intimate, and faithful. God calls out to us, inviting us to share in the divine life. How can we hear that call? What could hearing it mean as we live day to day? How can we help each other hear God's voice and follow where God leads? How do we open that reception room in our hearts?

This book explores the themes of call, discernment, and community as they relate to each other. It invites us to be aware of, and responsive to, our listening hearts. It is intended to help us recognize the risen Lord who abides with us. It encourages us to believe that as we hear God's call, we learn, step by step, to walk with the Lord. It reminds us that, in responding to God's call, we discover ourselves.

The title rises from the Hebrew-Christian tradition that understands the heart to have more than a physical nature, that sees the heart as the core of the person, at the center of the body, touching all of the body, mind, soul, and spirit.[2] Eastern Orthodox writers bid, "Let your mind descend into your heart."[3] When we draw together with truly listening hearts, we enter into communion with one another and with God.

Learning to listen within our hearts may not come easily. We muse, Does God call ordinary people like us? And if so, to what? How can we distinguish God's voice from all of the other voices that clamor at us—those of our culture, peer pressure, our careers, our egos? Amid our secular lives, where can we find support for our calls? And how can we remain faithful and accountable?

Christians have always struggled to understand what God would have them do. In 1835, Søren Kierkegaard wrote in his journal,

> What I really lack is to be clear in my mind *what I am to do, not* what I am to know. . . . The thing is to understand myself, to see what God really wishes *me* to do. . . . What good would it do me to be able to explain the meaning of Christianity if it had no deeper significance *for me and for my life?* [Emphasis in original][4]

For two years, a group of people studied the works of writers who, over the centuries, have considered similar questions. A smaller group met weekly using the model of the Quakers: beginning and ending in silence, listening to one another prayerfully, waiting for consensus to emerge. In this newly revised edition, the appendices of practical suggestions have been updated to reflect learnings that have come to Listening Hearts Ministries through 20 years of experience. Also, a glossary of discernment terms has been added after the annotated bibliography to provide a reference for people engaged in further reading, study, and discussion.

This book can be used for meditation. If a sentence or a phrase gives pause, it may be good to reflect on it. It may point to a place where God touches our lives—surely one that ought not be missed in haste.

The book can also be used as a basis for group discussion. By reading a designated chapter in advance and marking portions that speak to them, participants can pave the way for dialogue that touches their own experience.

Notes crediting sources and elaborating on thoughts in the book are placed at the end so as not to interfere with the flow of the text. The appendices set forth ways that groups can be formed to explore issues of call and support for ministries.

'Come' my heart has said, 'Seek [the Lord's] presence.'
—Ps. 27:8 (REB)

CALL

ONE

What Is "Call" for the Christian?

... let each of you lead the life ... to which God called you.
–1 Cor. 7:17

People call us to get our attention, to make contact
with us, to draw us closer to them. So it is with God.
A call may come as a gradual dawning of God's purpose
for our lives. It can involve an accelerating sense of
inner direction. It can emerge through a gnawing
feeling that we need to do a specific thing. On occasion, it can burst forth as a sudden awareness of a path
that God would have us take. Call may be emphatic
and unmistakable, or it may be obscure and subtle.[1] In
whatever way call is experienced, through the centuries
God has chosen to speak to us and bids us to listen. "I
will instruct you and teach you the way you should go;
I will counsel you with my eye upon you" (Ps. 32:8).

God calls us on many levels: God calls creation, calls
the Church, calls my congregation, and calls me,

today, to reach me where I am now. God calls the entirety of my life. And at specific times and places, God calls me to particular actions.

God calls each of us. There are a variety of calls, and no one call is inherently better or higher than any other. The call of a priest, monk, or nun, however sacred, is, in and of itself, not superior to the call of an architect designing a house, a mechanic repairing a car, or a nurse caring for the sick.[2] It is our faithfulness to God and not our station in life that honors a call.[3]

We need to look beneath external facts to determine a call. For example, two men might be wrestling with what seems to be the same question: whether or not to volunteer at a breakfast program for homeless people. For one, the call might turn out to be to stay home and spend some much-needed time with his children. For the other, the call might be to work at the breakfast program and help his family develop a sense of supporting him in service to others.

God speaks to us through the language of everyday events.[4] Each new moment of life, each new situation, the present condition of a person or community, of events, time, place, people, and circumstances—all hold clues to God's call.[5] Thus, we often find our calls in the facts, circumstances, and concrete experiences of daily life.[6]

Sometimes call comes through what is imposed on us. Teresa of Avila, for instance, wrote several books because her confessors told her to. Today, with hind-sight, we can recognize that through her obedience she was honoring God's call. Similarly, Dietrich Bonhoeffer found in prison a call to minister to others who were imprisoned.

Any matter, large or small, may relate to our call. A call could encompass a decision about whether to take a new job, go back to school, volunteer at a shelter. A call could draw us to a personal relation-ship in a new or different way. A call could focus on whether to resist paying taxes as a form of protest or whether to sell all our belongings and move to Central America. A call may not be so much a call to "do" as to "be." An active man may become sick and unable to do what he has done before; yet while he may not be called to be sick, he may be called in sickness to reflect God's presence and love in a new way. So call should be understood in the widest, most inclusive sense, to encompass what we do and who we are.

This is not to say that in every decision there is a call from God or that God is always giving us guidance regarding every question we face. Sometimes we need to act based upon our assessment of what is good—we need to make a decision. In such a situation, elevating the decision to a call from God will not make it one.[7]

On the other hand, because a matter seems unimport-ant does not foreclose a call from God. As with God's call to Moses, the desire to minister at a soup kitchen or as a school volunteer can burn brightly with the fire of God's call.

A call might lead us to pursue a certain occupation or career, as a person who feels called to help others in turmoil might become a pastoral counselor. Quite often a call becomes visible in a specific job, task, or endeavor. But a call can never be reduced to such activities. The same counselor may also be called to care for family, friends, and community as well as clients and thus must balance all of these in order to be faithful to the call. In a world that puts much emphasis on success, a too-narrow concern with occupation or career can make us deaf to our calls.[8]

We may be called beyond ordinary occupations—to be prophets. A prophet does not have to be a Moses or a Jeremiah. Amos, for example, was a shepherd who left his flock to become a prophet in Israel, returning home when his years of prophesying came to an end. So, too, any one of us may be called to a prophetic role at a specific time and place for a specific issue.

Not only is every call unique, but the hearing of every call is unique also. One sign that God may be calling is a certain restlessness, a certain dissatisfaction with things as they are. Other signs of God's call may be a sense of longing, yearning, or wondering; a feeling of being at a crossroads; a sense that something is happening in one's life, that one is wrestling with an issue or decision; a sense of being in a time of transition; or a series of circumstances that draw one into a specific issue.

While role models are helpful, we are not called to copy other people.[9] Rather, we are to become fully the people God created us to be, living our own lives in response to our own calls—as Jesus lived out his life faithful to God's call for him.[10] So it is that hearing one's call is akin to discovering one's self.[11]

Even when a need exists and we are well qualified to meet it, we are not necessarily called to respond to it. Something may seem logical for us to do, but that does not mean that God calls us to do it. In ordinary circumstances, people analyze facts in order to come to a conclusion. While this is a useful exercise, it is not the same thing as discerning God's call.

> This is the irrational season
> When love blooms bright and wild.
> Had Mary been filled with reason
> There'd have been no room for the child.[12]

Ultimately, it is not what the evidence suggests but the source of the call that gives it authority.

Similarly, simply because a task or undertaking is good to do does not mean that we are called to do it or that we should continue doing it. To be doing what is good can be the greatest obstacle to doing something even better.[13] We may understand only with hindsight why we were called to do something different.

Call usually involves service or benefit to others. In fact, a sense of call may be suspect if it does not involve service.[14] Nonetheless, the fruits of call are sometimes a long time in coming;[15] indeed, we may never perceive them. Things we say or do can have a profound impact we may never know about. Sometimes the fruits of our life manifest themselves at a much later time, perhaps even after our death.[16] The Letter to the Hebrews reminds us of this in its account of Abraham and Sarah:

> By faith Abraham obeyed when he was called to set out for a place that he was to receive as an inheritance; and he set out, not knowing where he was going. By faith he stayed for a time in the Land he had been promised. . . . By faith he received power of procreation, even though he was too old—and Sarah herself was barren—because he considered him faithful who had promised.
>
> All of these died in faith without having received the promises, but from a distance they saw and greeted them. (Heb. 11:8, 9, 11, 13)

Every true call is a call to obey God; indeed, the word *obedience* derives from the Latin *audire*, which means "to listen."[17] Jesus came to include us in his divine obedience,[18] saying, "If you love me, you will keep my commandments" (John 14:15), and "They who have my commandments and keep them are those who love me . . ." (John 14:21). If we love God, we want to live in harmony with God—we want to hear what God has to say, and we want to act on what we hear. St. Paul refers to this as "obedient from the heart" (Rom. 6:17).

While call requires response and obedience, we will not be given a road map. Our response to a call is not mechanical application. Rather, call requires that we take responsibility. We will not necessarily be called to come up with a correct answer, as in a crossword puzzle, but something freer and more creative. We are given building blocks to see what can be done with them, using for the task all of our intelligence, creativity, sensitivity, and love. Our critical faculties are required; we must use them the best way we can, constructively and with love.[19]

Awareness of a call may give rise to a feeling of inadequacy, as illustrated in the classical biblical calls of Moses, Jeremiah, and Isaiah. Moses said no five times to God (Exod. 3:11, 13; 4:1, 10, 13). Moses' excuses included not knowing God's name, not being a person of consequence, not having credibility, and not being a good speaker. Jeremiah responded to God, "Ah, Lord God! Truly I do not know how to speak, for I am only a boy" (Jer. 1:6). Before Isaiah could say, "Here I am," in response to God's call, he expressed his profound sense of unworthiness with the cry, "I am a man of unclean lips" (Isa. 6:5).

Yet God not only calls but empowers—although the power may come only as we respond. Conversely, if we don't respond to God's call, we may cut ourselves off from the Lord's strength and become increasingly blind and deaf to God's promptings. To ignore or resist a call may "fracture us further, widening the split between what we subscribe to inwardly and what we do outwardly."[20]

Our calls are always evolving. If we are to respond, we need to listen, not only today but as today evolves into tomorrow. In times of transition, we need to listen with extra care. "If we go on listening, we feel God pulling us, drawing us into another current, a larger, deeper, stronger one than our usual little force."[21]

> *Morning by morning he wakens—*
> *wakens my ear*
> *to listen as those who are taught.*
> *The Lord God has opened my ear. . . .*
> *-Isa. 50:4–5*

TWO

Call to Ministry

*Jesus said to them . . . "As the Father has sent me,
so I send you." —John 20:21*

Ministry is the active response to God's call. Christian
ministry is more than simply doing good. Rather, it is
something that Christ does in us and through us and
that we do in and through Christ.[1] As ministers of state
act not on their own but on the authority of the states
that send them, so, too, we act not on our own but on
the authority of God who calls us. Jesus said, "You did
not choose me, but I chose you. And I appointed you to
go and bear fruit, fruit that will last . . ." (John 15:16).

Ministry comes from the same root as *minus*, which
means "less." Jesus said, "For who is greater: the one
who is at the table or the one who serves? Is it not
the one at the table? But I am among you as one who
serves" (Luke 22:27). Paul, too, reminds us that our

Lord "did not count equality with God as a thing to be grasped, but emptied himself, taking the form of a servant" (Phil. 2:6-7; RSV). Our call, then, will place us in the role of a minister, on God's behalf, in service to God's creation.

We do not need to be ordained to have a ministry. *The Book of Common Prayer* specifies, "The ministers of the Church are lay persons, bishops, priests, and deacons."[2] All Christians are called to minister both to one another and to those around them by participating in God's work in the world. Ministry can occur between child and parent; among workers in an office or factory; between neighbors and friends. Hospitality may be ministry: welcoming the stranger, receiving and treating the people we encounter each day warmly and generously. Ministry includes prayer for one another. Ministry occurs in innumerable forms, some of which require ordination.

A minister is also one who waits, ready to respond as called. A waiter serves not only when running to the kitchen but also while waiting attentively. In this spirit, we await God's call to act in service to others.

Genuine ministry involves both giving and receiving. This reciprocity is central. Ministry "to" is patronizing, for it fails to acknowledge our own need; nor does it recognize the mutual nurturing experienced when we are brought to Christ through the people we serve. Those who minister at a soup kitchen, for example, often find themselves deeply enriched by those they serve.

Doing good things—volunteer work, for instance—may not be ministry if God is not the motivating force—even if the person doing them is a Christian.[3] On the other hand, if God is the motivating force, even those who do not consciously bear the name of Christ may participate in God's work. God used Cyrus, king of Persia, to release Israel from captivity, saying, ". . . I call you by your name, I surname you, though you do not know me" (Isa. 45:4). One task of the Christian, then, is to recognize, affirm, and celebrate Christ's reconciling action in others, including non-Christians. A true minister is "anybody who is the channel to others of God's love, and is willing to share something of the cost of that love; and whose eyes are open to perceive God's presence everywhere and in everybody."[4]

> *Whoever serves me must follow me, and where*
> *I am, there will my servant be also. . . .*
> *—John 12:26*

DISCERNMENT

THREE

What Is Discernment?

Beloved, do not believe every spirit, but test the spirits to see whether they are from God. . . . –1 John 4:1

Discernment comes from the Latin word *discernere*, which means "to separate," "to distinguish," "to determine," "to sort out." In classical spirituality, discernment means identifying what spirit is at work in a situation: the Spirit of God or some other spirit. Discernment is "sifting through" our interior and exterior experiences to determine their origin.[1] Discernment helps a person understand the source of a call, to whom it is directed, its content, and what response is appropriate. Discernment also involves learning if one is dodging a call, is deaf to a call, or is rejecting a call.

Discernment is a gift from God.[2] But it also includes an intentional attempt on our part to hear God's call in our life.[3] It takes work; it is also a matter of grace. It involves our full humanity as well as communion with God.

Many voices call us: voices of culture, career, upbringing, worldview, peer pressure, ego, self-interest. These voices may be good in and of themselves yet may drown out the voice of God. How can we distinguish between God's call and other calls? How can we evaluate whether a call springs from a desire for security or comfort or success, rather than from God? How can we verify that a call comes from God?

No rules provide definitive answers to these questions.[4] And some rules that do exist provide poor or incomplete guidance. The experiences of the early Quakers illustrate this. One test some Quaker sects used to confirm God's call was that a "true" call was always contrary to one's own will.[5] The assumption that a "cross to the will"[6] meant taking up the cross of Christ often produced absurd results. For example, some Friends walked naked in the streets because it was "contrary to [their] own will or inclination" and, therefore, "in obedience to the Lord."[7] Another test was reliance on a selected passage of Scripture. Frequently, however, this meant (and can still mean) merely choosing some biblical passages and ignoring others to confirm a precharted course.[8]

The ability to discern comes from living the life of the Spirit, a process of growth involving an ever-greater integration of desires, feelings, reactions, and choices with a continuing commitment to abide in Christ. Indeed, through integrating the actions and relationships of life into one's identity with Christ we come to feel whether various impulses move us toward or away from the Spirit.[9] The ability to discern develops in a relationship with God, as one becomes rooted and grounded in the heart of God.[10] Thus, people who abide in the Lord are more likely to be able to hear and distinguish calls.[11]

As we move toward spiritual maturity, we move beyond the need for specific rules and answers into the darkness of God where we must act in faith rather than certainty. In discernment we move through and beyond our feelings, our thoughts, and our reasoning about what God wants of us, to be led by God's Spirit toward action. Discernment does not imply fully comprehending God's will,[12] but rather it raises the question, What is the next step God wants me to take?[13]

Discernment may be understood as "apprehending" rather than "comprehending."[14] Although discernment involves use of reason, the process is delicate and easily stifled by excessive analysis.[15] Pascal observes, "The heart has its reasons, that reason does not know."[16] Discernment of call involves intuition and insight, ". . . for that which has not been told them, they shall see, and that which they have not heard, they shall understand" (Isa. 52:15; RSV). As we respond in faith and action, we gain insight.

When we turn our hearts to God, we experience a reorientation of values deep within us. To paraphrase Jan Wood's address to the Friends' Consultation on Discernment, one of two things may happen. Either we become increasingly astute and wise as we live out our new orientation—we walk in the Spirit. Or, if we are not true to the new life that is rising within us—if we deny, repress, or live in contradiction to it—we invite internal havoc and trigger war within ourselves. Our lives may take on a frantic quality.[17]

Because the evidence and experiences on which we act are usually conflicting and ambivalent, and because we are by nature vulnerable to our capacity for self-deception, discernment is often tentative and uncertain.[18] We may not feel a great sense of having found the truth. Discernment can be like driving an automobile at night: the headlights cast only enough light for us to see the next small bit of road immediately in front of us.[19] Ultimately, discernment requires our willingness to act in faith on our sense of what God wants us to do.[20]

We need to risk making mistakes. We can dare to make mistakes because we know that God has forgiven us when we are wrong.[21] What is important is that we act on what we have discerned. In obedience to discernment, more discernment will come.[22] We need to be attentive and alert in order to hear and understand God's call and then act, knowing that God blesses even our mistakes.

> *. . . the word is very near you; it is in your mouth and in*
> *your heart, so that you can do it.*
> *–Deut. 30:14 (RSV)*

FOUR

What Conditions Help Discern God's Call?

. . . turn to the Lord your God with all your heart and with all your soul. –Deut. 30:10

God speaks, touches, and reveals in God's own way and in God's own time. Still, the presence of certain conditions, such as trust, prayer, and patience, makes discernment of God's call more likely.[1] Having or meeting these conditions does not mean that we *will* discern God's call, only that discernment becomes more likely.[2]

The conditions in this chapter apply not only to a person seeking discernment but to all who are trying to help that person. It is God's call, not mere decision-making, that we seek.[3] In order to discern which path is authentic, all involved need to desire to know God, to be willing to be pervaded by God's presence.

We need to go through a process that cleanses our vision to see what is true and frees our will to act on what we see.[4] Here are some ways we may prepare to hear God's call.

TRUST

> "Commit your way to the Lord; trust in him, and he will act." (Ps. 37:5)

First and foremost, we have to be willing to trust God and one another. Trust that God is present to us, speaks to us, is loving and merciful, and has work for us to do.[5] Trust that, in opening our hearts to others, we will encounter the Lord.[6] We need to act on the conviction that "all things work together for good for those who love God" (Rom. 8:28).

LISTENING

> "O that my people would listen to me, that Israel would walk in my ways!" (Ps. 81:13)

Discernment involves listening. We must listen with open hearts and open minds,[7] especially to what we do not want to hear.[8] If discernment is to take place, we must let go of our preconceptions and expectations.[9] We must be willing to hear the appealing and the unappealing, the familiar and the unfamiliar. If we become selective, we may turn a deaf ear to God.

We need to listen with our bodies as well as with our minds, for God speaks to us through our pains and pleasures, through our wills, emotions, and senses.[10] To hear, we must listen with every fiber of our being.[11]

We must listen in silence, for stillness and silence enable us to hear. Elijah did not hear God in the mighty wind or in the earthquake or in the fire but in a still, small voice (1 Kings 19:11-13).

PRAYER

> "Seek the Lord and his strength; seek his presence continually." (Ps. 105:4)

Typically, we think of prayer as what we say to God, as in petition or in thanksgiving. Unlike the boy, Samuel, who said, "Speak, Lord, for your servant listens" (1 Sam. 3:10),[12] we often pray, "Listen, Lord, for your servant speaks." But prayer, especially prayer for discernment, involves listening. Through prayer we seek for ourselves total attentiveness to the all-embracing presence of Christ. For Christ is found in the circumstances, the people, the things of daily life.[13] If we are aware of this, we will open our hearts, and, in this way, our whole life can become prayer in action.

KNOWLEDGE OF SCRIPTURE

> "If you continue in my word . . . you will know the truth." (John 8:31-32)

Scripture is central to discerning call. The Bible records centuries of the developing historical and spiritual relationship between God and the people of God. The more familiar we are with Scripture, the more ready our access to the experience of God's people in history. Moreover, as the living Word of God, Scripture continues to communicate to us.

HUMILITY

> "He leads the humble in what is right, and teaches the humble his way." (Ps. 25:9)

Humility derives ultimately from the same root as *humus*, meaning ground or earth. An attitude of humility is rooted in a true sense of one's self. Humility, grounded in self-knowledge, helps us to avoid the distortions of both inordinate self-confidence and exaggerated self-doubt.[14] A humble person is not someone who feels inferior but someone who is without pretense, down to earth. Humility lays the foundation for discernment because to be "humble in heart," as Jesus instructs us (Matt. 11:29), means that we will accept the uniqueness of our experience and the limited nature of our knowledge.[15] An attitude of humility allows us to accept dependence on God and one another and to be open to God's turning us in a new or unexpected direction.

Humility is not gained by seeking it directly nor obtained by focusing on one's faults and sins. Rather, it comes quietly to those who draw close to the Lord. As we experience God's greatness, we sense our own smallness. When we encounter God's wholeness, we realize our own incompleteness.[16]

DISCIPLINE AND PERSEVERANCE

> "Those who seek me diligently find me."
> (Prov. 8:17)

It is all but essential for us to set aside a time and place to be in solitude so that we can be receptive to God's presence through Scripture, prayer, and silence.[17] This requires perseverance, especially for those who are not naturally inclined to solitude.[18]

PATIENCE AND URGENCY

> "Be still before the Lord, and wait patiently. . . ."
> (Ps. 37:7)

Remember, it is God's call, not our call. So we need to be content to incline our ears with patience. In the meantime, let us offer up our prayers to God, asking God repeatedly to nurture our faith.

Still, while patience is called for at times, a sense of urgency is sometimes imperative. C.S. Lewis warns against progressing quietly and comfortably toward hell.[19]

"But everything has its time, and the main thing is that we keep step with God, and do not keep pressing on a few steps ahead—nor keep dawdling a step behind."[20]

PERSPECTIVE

> "Is it lawful to heal on the sabbath?" (Matt. 12:10, RSV)

Do not make an idol of discernment. "The only priority worth having is knowing and loving God. Stay in the space of Love. Do not be lured out of it."[21] If discernment follows, fine; if not, so be it. Let it rest lightly. "Release your discernment from your ego and your expectations. Flow as a stream that is useful to those who can take" from it and is "in no way diminished by those who can't."[22]

At the same time, "Be true to what is inside. Put weight on it. Live by it. Hold it with sufficient tentativeness to be open to others . . . and with sufficient tenacity to live it out until moved differently."[23]

Impediments

Just as there are conditions favorable to discernment, there are impediments. Everything that gets in the way of hearing God's call is a barrier: "They served their idols, which became a snare to them" (Ps. 106:36). Obstacles arise from:

- *Culture*. Cultural values emphasizing competition, success, productivity, self-sufficiency, individualism, or material progress may impede discernment.

- *Prosperity*. Prosperity knits a person to the world.[24] "I spoke to you in your prosperity, but you said, 'I will not listen'" (Jer. 22:21).

- *Self-interest*. We need to free ourselves from the trap of self-interest that so grasps and clutches that it gets in the way of a free and open relationship with God and with others.[25] God begins where clinging to things ends.[26]

- *Self-absorption*. Ambition and self-absorption obstruct discernment.

- *Self-righteousness*. To be sure we are living in God's light is a sign of spiritual smugness and an impediment to discerning God's call.[27]

- *Desire for security*. Our desire for security and control interferes with our ability to hear God's call.

• *Desire for certainty*. To insist on an exact answer diminishes our freedom to listen.[28]

• *Human time frames*. Our own timetables impair our ability to let God point the way.

• *Self-doubt*. If we do not think we are good enough, we may not believe we can be useful to God and may be unable to pursue God's call. Moses was fortunate that God would not accept his response of personal inadequacy. We need to act on our best understanding of what God wants, praying that God will correct us if we have been misunderstood.

And so, as we move from self-will to God's will, we place our lives in the hands of God. And then we find that God has work for us to do.

> *. . . you will find him if you search after him with all your heart and soul. –Deut. 4:29*

FIVE

Is It God We Are Hearing?

*Give your servant a heart to understand how to discern
between good and evil. –1 Kings 3:9 (JB)*

Access to what has been true for others can help us
to evaluate whether what we hear and see comes
from God. The following insights are derived from
the experience of Christians from varying traditions
whose lives collectively span the centuries.

WHERE TO LOOK

"Seeking God does not demand the unusual, the
spectacular, the heroic."[1] It is in the here and now,
the ordinary situation of normal life, that we find
God. A true call is likely to be modest in scope. If we
try to save the world, we become immobilized.[2]

Our Own Lives

There are stories from our lives through which God is trying to tell us things we need to know. We need to identify those stories, tell them, and try to sort them out. We need "to read our own history, to see the turning points, the moments of change, the unfolding of God's plan for us at each new step of the way."[3]

By observing what we do, we can discover what we believe and value. Our past actions, our previous choices, the roads we have taken—all hold clues to who we are becoming. There is a connection between our temperaments and talents, and our call. We are called to work with the gifts we have been given. For this reason it is important to know our gifts. Paul warns, "Do not neglect the gift that is in you" (1 Tim. 4:14). Teilhard de Chardin suggests that when trying to draw out the full potential of a person, it is important to tap into those qualities that are unique.[4]

Still, discerning God's call is not the same as identifying one's gifts.[5] Unwilling to confront Pharaoh, Moses protested that he was not an eloquent speaker (Exod. 4:10). Yet God called Moses, saying, "Now go, I shall help you to speak and tell you what to say" (Exod. 4:12, JB). In discerning call, we need to be open to what Dag Hammarskjöld calls the "way of possibility,"[6] for we may not assess our gifts accurately, may not understand what is needed, may not see as God sees.[7]

The Desire for Change

Stability and change are factors to consider in discernment. Stability requires that we not run away from the place our battles are being fought.[8] If we cannot find God where we are, we may not be able to find God elsewhere.[9] Yet we need to be open to change. The call to change is ultimately nothing more and nothing less than a commitment to follow wherever Christ leads.[10]

There is an ebb and flow to life and work; at times our tasks are hard and difficult, at other times light and free. A long period of time during which our burdens are only heavy, when there is only ebb and no flow, may be a sign that we need to clarify our call. It may mean we are missing what God wants us to do amid the many things we are doing. If a call is a true call, we usually do not get burned out. A true call tends to be energizing.

It is important to know, however, that a person can be led by God into what John of the Cross calls a "dark night of the soul," a spiritual experience marked by great distress and prolonged tribulation.[11] Some of the signs of the Spirit seem to be absent. Yet other signs of the Spirit are present, though possibly difficult to see in the darkness. A person going through this kind of an experience needs to seek out someone with skill in this area.[12]

Assessing the Options

To consult moral rules such as those contained in the Ten Commandments can provide guidance, not to crush inner promptings and not to take their place, but to test them.[13] However, pride can make us cling to our understanding of a moral rule.[14] Thus, while moral rules provide capsules of wisdom tested by time, we must resist treating them as idols.[15]

It can be helpful to examine our ideas against opposing ideas. For example, if we feel a desire to do something, it can help to consider likely consequences were we to do the opposite.[16] Bear in mind that what could be a good decision for one person might be the wrong one for someone else.[17] What might be the right choice at one time could be the wrong one at another time.

God's purpose is unified. If it seems that God's messages are contradictory, we need to view the situation from a different or wider angle or step back to find a new vantage point. Still, it is good to be mindful that God's ways are not our ways (Isa. 55:8), and God may be calling us to act in a way we do not understand.[18]

The Needs of Others

In baptism we are incorporated into the Body of Christ, which makes us communal by definition. To quote Paul, "together [we] make a unity . . . building up the body of Christ" (Eph. 4:13, JB). Thus, the needs of the community are important to consider in evaluating a call.

Jesus frequently chose the humble, poor, rejected, and despised. They are often the preferred dwelling place of God—in them, we may meet God.[19] If we are hearing something that leads us to the disadvantaged, it may be a good indication that God is trying to get our attention.

> If you take away from the midst of you the yoke, the pointing of the finger . . . if you pour yourself out for the hungry and satisfy the desire of the afflicted, then shall your light rise in the darkness and your gloom be as the noonday. And the Lord will guide you continually. (Isa. 58:911, RSV)

SCRIPTURE

When we think that our Lord is speaking to us, it is prudent to determine if what we hear is consistent with Scripture.[20] If it is not, perhaps the voice we hear is not God's. Or, if it is God, we may be misunderstanding what is being said. Or we may be misinterpreting Scripture.

We need to bear in mind that every word spoken in the Bible is a partial and limited witness to truth.[21] We should not let our preferences silence any biblical voice, nor should we read the Bible merely to assure ourselves that we are right but, rather, to look for areas in which we have not been listening.[22] Take care to consider the context in which a book of Scripture was written. Accepting a passage of Scripture without considering its presuppositions can lead to distortion.[23]

While each generation must preserve the teaching that has been passed on, it must also add to this living tradition its own experience of Christ.[24] No one can hear the gospel of Christ except through the events of one's own time, for the Holy Spirit is a living teacher who does not merely repeat a tradition of the past.[25] Thus, it is good to beware of legalism and authoritarianism, always listening anew for the voice of Christ.

MOTIVES

A healthy skepticism of our own motives is a sign of spiritual maturity. For instance, many Christians have vied for the privilege of presiding at eucharist. Would they be so likely to vie to wash dirty feet?[26] We need to examine our motives for wanting to serve in a specific way. Christ's false friends are those who consider themselves his friends but who go about seeking Jesus for their own satisfaction.[27]

SIGNS OF GOD'S CALL

God often speaks through signs. No single sign ensures that a particular understanding of God's will is correct. Neither is it likely that all signs will be present in any given situation. Nevertheless, signs can combine to provide an informed sense of where the Spirit is pointing. Some signs to watch for:

• Peace—the central sign. Peace does not mean an absence of trouble. Rather, it means a firm conviction, even in the midst of turmoil, that *the Lord is risen* and that "all shall be well."[28] Serenity is its manifestation. But beware of false peace. This can come from escaping an unhappy situation, denying painful realities, avoiding a cross, or making a decision (even one that is wrong) merely to terminate a crisis of indecision. If the peace endures through ups and downs, then we have confirmation that it is authentic.[29]

• Joy—a deep interior joy that is unselfconscious and uninhibited.[30]

• A temporary experience of disorientation, followed by calm and serenity.[31]

• Tears that are comforting and tranquilizing, rather than disturbing and fatiguing.[32]

• A sudden sense of clarity.

• Strands of experience that seemed unrelated begin to converge and fit together.

• Persistence—the message keeps recurring through different channels.

Through integrating our desires, feelings, reactions, and choices with our life in God, we may come to sense whether or not various impulses are from God. This experiential knowledge and the clarity that accompanies it are known as "felt-knowledge."[33]

God's call may be heard through a spiritual experience. The experience may be unsought and unexpected but vivid and indelible.[34] It is so clear at the time it occurs that we would not think to question it.[35] At first it may leave us speechless, but later able to speak of it. It is attended by gratitude, love, and humility. A spiritual experience may include an image from God that lasts only an instant but is branded in us forever.[36]

Circumstance and coincidence may cause us to be in the right place at the right time to do God's work in a specific way. This may be a sign that God is calling us. So, too, if we seem to be the only ones aware of a concern and wonder why someone does not do something, it may be that we are being called to do it.

CAUTIONS

It is not possible to help everybody. Being endlessly available to anyone or everyone is good for no one.[37]

In times of inner turmoil, disturbance, sadness, or depression, be wary of making a change. Move slowly and carefully, for in such a time the way to a right decision can be obscured.[38]

Previous commitments demand serious consideration. Commitments generally, and especially commitments to children, spouse, and others, must be a factor in determining God's call and the timing and nature of one's response.[39] Watch out for feelings of peace that come from escape, even when accompanied by feelings of joy.[40]

Avoid being dominated by human timetables; it is God's time, not our time, that is our concern. If we are anxious or obsessed about the future, it is a sign that we may be out of touch with God's presence. In contrast, confidence in the future based on trust in God frees us to live fully in the present.[41]

The presence of fervor and passion for a particular path is not necessarily trustworthy—unless the zeal emanates from love of God. The real test is not how much we want to do something but how much love is a part of what we want to do.

A call may seem perfectly reasonable, but neither is this trustworthy. We must remember that we can deceive ourselves by reasoning.[42] Coming to a carefully reasoned conclusion does not mean we have discerned God's call.

We should beware of certainty, arrogance, and thoughts of superiority. Those who are positive about what is true may very well be deceived.[43]

If the apparent good that comes to us is accompanied by vanity, anxiety, irritability, resentment, condemnation, or condescension, it may be a sign that we are not hearing God's call.[44]

It is important to realize that the devil can operate in very subtle ways, appealing to our sense of what is good. One way to describe evil is as "segmented good." This suggests that we can be tempted to concentrate on one thing that is good while ignoring what is best for the whole.

You will know them by their fruits.
–Matt. 7:16

COMMUNITY

SIX

Why Is Christian Community Important in Discerning God's Call?

Where two or three are gathered in my name, there am I in the midst of them. –Matt. 18:20 (RSV)

Jesus lived his life in common with others, sharing and participating in God's work. He began his ministry by calling Simon, Andrew, and others to proclaim the Good News (Matt. 4:18-22; Mark 1:16-20). During his ministry he continued to gather men and women, and he ended his ministry by promising to be with them always (Matt. 28:16-20).

As followers of Jesus, we are called to live as Jesus did: in a community of faith. The word *community* comes from *communis*, meaning "common," and from *communicare*, meaning "to share or participate." Paul uses the metaphor of the Body of Christ to describe the interconnectedness of all members: "Now you are the body of Christ and individually members of it . . ." (1 Cor. 12:27). "If one member suffers, all suffer together with it; if one member is honored, all rejoice together with it" (1 Cor. 12:26). A life lived in common faith with others—in community—is central to Christianity.

God seeks a personal relationship with each of us and solitude is vital to our life in God. Jesus himself often went to a quiet place, alone, to pray (Mark 1:35; 6:46; 14:32-39). Yet Scripture makes a special point of bidding us to come together in God's name. Jesus said, "Where two or three are gathered in my name, there am I in the midst of them" (Matt. 18:20, RSV).

Something happens to us when we consult one another in Christian community.[1] In sharing our thoughts with others, surprising insights often emerge—opening our eyes to what we have not seen and our ears to what we have not heard.[2] This can transform and liberate us beyond our own narrow expectations. Both the one experiencing a call and those helping that person may express God's wisdom and grace in the process. "I will give you shepherds after my own heart, who will feed you with knowledge and understanding" (Jer. 3:15).

Although God calls each of us personally, as individuals we see only partially. Individual perception, reasoning, and understanding are always limited. Even a person who feels absolutely certain that a specific revelation comes from God may be mistaken as to how it is to be applied.[3] Because God often reveals part of the picture to one person and another part to another person, it is prudent to consult one another to discern God's counsel, guidance, and direction, even if there is no apparent reason to do so.[4] While circumstances sometimes require us to act without consulting others, the danger of arrogance and error in proceeding on our own can be great.[5]

Another role for community is all but essential in order for us to recognize and respond to our call. It is to encourage us in our love of God and to keep us from becoming conformed to the world. How are we to resist the powerful attraction of the world's values: love of money, power, social approval, security, comfort, success? For many of us, the answer is only by meeting together regularly in the name of the Lord, probably in small groups, and thereby experiencing God's presence and love. In this company, in the light and presence of Christ, we can see through the sham of worldly values yet share in God's love for all creation. In this company, we are strengthened to live as God's people. Here, we can perceive truth and be obedient and faithful to our call in spite of the pull of the world.

Just hours before his death, Jesus prayed for his disciples:

> Holy Father, protect them in your name that you have given me, so that they may be one, as we are one. . . . I have given them your word, and

the world has hated them because they do not belong to the world, just as I do not belong to the world. I am not asking you to take them out of the world, but I ask you to protect them from the evil one. They do not belong to the world, just as I do not belong to the world. Sanctify them in the truth; your word is truth. As you have sent me into the world, so I have sent them into the world. And for their sakes I sanctify myself, so that they also may be sanctified in truth. (John 17:11, 14–19)

By meeting together in the Lord's name, we claim that prayer for ourselves. And we can accept truth and God's call for us without being overwhelmed by the judgment and values of the world.

Nevertheless, we should bear in mind that from the very start our Christian communities have had their weaknesses as well as strengths, their errors as well as insights. Thus, advice, judgment, and support from a community must be received critically, as well as with love and respect. This can be particularly evident when a person in the community feels called to a prophetic role.

The prophet is not an easy person for the community to accept. It can be a trial for a community to hear the prophet's voice and acknowledge that it comes from God, since the very task of the prophet is to challenge the status quo. A hundred years before the

Civil War, John Woolman felt called to be an abolitionist among the Quakers, but he also felt that he should not undertake this without the blessing of his Meeting.[6] As a result, Woolman wrestled with his faith community over this issue for two years; many members of the community owned slaves. While many did not agree with the abolitionist position, they came to believe that Woolman did have a call and promised to support him and his family while he responded to it. During the two years Woolman stayed and presented his call, the community's members were deeply affected. Because of Woolman's faithfulness to his call and willingness to work out that call in the community, the Quakers eventually came to oppose slavery.[7]

We can never achieve wholeness simply by ourselves but only together with others.[8] Consequently, as we involve the community in discerning call, God enlivens and strengthens both us and the community.

> ... the saints together make a unity in the work of
> service, building up the body of Christ.
> -Eph. 4:13 (JB)

SEVEN

The Value of a Discernment Group

Let us consider how to stir up one another to love and good works, not neglecting to meet together. . . but encouraging one another. –Heb. 10:24-25 (RSV)

As our life in God deepens, and our knowledge of call and discernment broadens, we may find ourselves helping each other wrestle with issues of call when gathered informally. Likewise, groups meeting for specific purposes such as Bible study may at times focus on a question of call for one of the members. The more a Christian community becomes grounded in prayer and discernment, the more this kind of discussion will take place spontaneously.

Even so, some people will find it easier to get the kind of help they need if the community offers a specific structure, as described in appendix 1.

Whether a group is formal or informal, spontaneous or structured, it can help to consider how to proceed.

First, people seeking help need to provide some information about their own faith journeys. God communicates with each of us in a way that is unique. The more fully we can delineate patterns of God's communication over the span of our lives, the more effectively we can evaluate what is transpiring at the moment.

Once the person asking guidance has laid out the issues and sketched in the appropriate background, those present need to identify their own biases relative to the situation. We all have histories that shape our outlooks. What we have to say needs to be understood against the background of those histories. Ideally, each person present will silently reflect on questions such as these: What colors my perception of this person or issue? Would it be constructive for me to articulate my bias? We are more receptive to God's Spirit in an atmosphere that is honest and open, relaxed and gentle.

An additional consideration: we normally relate to some people in a group more readily than to others. Psychologically, we tend to turn off the people we most need to hear.[1] The people to whom we are least attracted often have the most to teach us. If we identify those to whom we are least drawn, we can make a special effort to listen to them attentively.

Prayerful listening may be the most important aspect of discernment. Paul Tillich wrote, "No human relation, especially no intimate one, is possible without mutual listening."[2] In the same way, no relationship with God, especially not an intimate one, is possible without mutual listening. As we listen to God in prayer and through one another, we grow in Christian community and in our sense of God's path for us.[3]

The silence of prayerful listening is not so much the absence of talk as it is presence to the Word. "We keep silence solely for the sake of the Word . . . to honor and receive it."[4] Frequent times of silence are important during a discernment gathering:

> There is a wonderful power of clarification, purification, and concentration upon the essential thing in being quiet. . . . This is true as a purely secular fact. But silence before the Word leads to right hearing, and thus also to right speaking of the Word of God at the right time.[5]

Members of the group help the person seeking discernment by listening prayerfully and raising questions concerning the issue. Prayerfully formulated questions invite the movement of God's Spirit. While there may be no clear answers, the right question can be crucial. Answers can shut down growth; good questions encourage growth. Answers sometimes terminate our listening; questions stimulate further listening.

A goal of a discernment group is to reach spiritual consensus, which the Quakers call "sense of the meeting." For the Quakers, this consensus is a way of sensing the will of God.[6] Spiritual consensus incorporates rational consideration, but comes most especially through prayerful listening.[7]

Consensus is not the same as unanimity, and it is not group decision making. Not everyone must actually agree, but no one can be so opposed as to feel obligated to resist. Since anyone can block consensus, the process gives each person power and requires each person to exercise that power responsibly.

When people feel a strong commitment to stand their ground, that desire compels them to reexamine their position and present it more clearly. Consensus relies on waiting prayerfully until everyone can find a position that all can embrace. No votes are taken. No one wins or loses.

In pursuing consensus, we have to try to build bridges and look for new ways to approach situations. We need to listen carefully to pinpoint areas of agreement and build on them. We need to look for ways to reconcile differing points of view, perhaps accommodating opposing sides of an issue. Efforts to arrive at consensus often produce unexpected results.

People meeting with a discernment group may come to feel that what they are hearing does not come from God. This, too, is discernment. For example, a person may unconsciously identify a course of action as coming from God in order to escape an intolerable situation. That person may come to understand that getting out of the situation is necessary but is not a call. Or a person may realize that certain decisions do not involve a call and simply need to be made. Or a consensus may emerge that a discernment group has gone far enough, leaving the issue of call to future resolution in God's own time. Understanding that a call does not come from God, or even seeing that an issue is not as clear as it once seemed, can quiet the cacophony within, creating stillness and space, fostering silent, listening hearts where, finally, we come to hear the Lord speak.

And so, as we help one another wrestle with issues of call, our knowledge of call and discernment broadens, and our life in God deepens.

Now the whole group of those who believed were of one heart and soul. . . . –Acts 4:32

EIGHT

Supporting the Ministries of Others

Moses' father-in-law said to him, "What you are doing is not good. You will surely wear yourself out, both you and these people with you. For the task is too heavy for you; you cannot do it alone." –Exod. 18:17-18

A wise swimmer does not cross a difficult channel without a boat close behind, with those aboard watching for signs of danger or weariness and providing words of encouragement along the way. Nor does a prudent climber scale a mountain alone, without companions to hold the rope and help along the way. Neither should one minister alone.

Ministry—lay or ordained—requires support. Without support, we may become lonely, bored, or weary. We may feel trapped by the tasks we have undertaken or find ourselves unable or unwilling to ask for help. Without support, ministry may become lost. Without support, we may become lost.

Whether support comes from a single person—a friend, companion, colleague, mentor, or adviser—or from a group, the key element is thoughtful attention. In order to respond to God's call effectively, we need time and occasions to talk about concerns and issues of vocation, to refine the call further, to be challenged, to be encouraged in a knowing and sustaining way, to be recognized, to be affirmed. Without time for talking, praying, and sharing, support can dwindle into superficial well-wishing or irrelevance or fade away altogether. Thus, the quality of the support we receive can make a vast difference as we face inevitable doubts, discouragements, and disappointments.

There are at least four ways to support and be supported in ministry: spiritually, psychologically, physically, and financially. The spiritual includes prayer, study of Scripture, and opportunities for reflection. The psychological involves affirming and understanding the person behind the ministry. The physical encompasses such diverse possibilities as offering a hug for encouragement or babysitting so that parents can pursue a particular ministry. The financial means putting our earthly treasure where our heart is—which is to say, funding ministry where funding is needed.

A person may find support in an existing group, such as one for Bible study, book discussion, or prayer. For example, if a sense of call arises from participation in a Bible study group, the relationships of trust and the shared commitments to Christian living within that group could provide a strong foundation for support. Indeed, a person in such a group may elicit the aid of the group when first embarking on discernment leading to ministry. Another person's sense of call might emerge from a group initiated to work through some crucial issue—illness, marriage or divorce, loss of or search for a job. That group's understanding of the person's struggle, motivations, and discoveries could provide a foundation for effective support of ministry.

In contrast, another person may be exercising a vocation with no group to support it. For this person, a separate group of people with similar ministries may be helpful. Support based on participation or experience in the same ministry can be effective, as colleagues can supply insights, empathy, and experiential knowledge that others, however well intentioned, cannot offer. A group of this kind might spring up naturally among people engaged in the same ministry: an emergency food or tutoring program, for example. The pattern is not identical for everyone, and the support group, whatever its origin, needs to listen closely to the different tones and overtones of call that may sound at different stages in a person's life.

A support group need not focus on a single person. For example, a group may find mutual support working on a single issue or complex of similar issues. Or a group may find ministry in their occupations and choose to meet to maintain a strong connection between their work and their faith. A mutual support group such as this has the added benefit of offering all members of the group the opportunity to provide as well as receive support.

Some may find their principal support coming from people or groups that have no connection with the church, in which case they will need to discover other ways to connect their ministry with the community of faith.

Support for ministry may take many forms, occur on different levels, come from various sources. But there must be support. If there is no existing form of support for a ministry or none readily available, a person called to that ministry needs to consult with the community to find support—ideally even before embarking on the ministry.[1]

Finally, in supporting ministry we need to be clear about just what is being supported—the person or the ministry. While personal issues and events have an inevitable impact on ministry, and while pastoral concern and attention are inseparable from support, the endeavor to support ministry is not meant to be therapy. The intention is to discover how to support a person in ministry, how to keep that ministry faithful to Christ's call.

We need to nurture the Christ in each person— individually, in small groups, and as responsible members of the larger Body of Christ. Ideally, support for ministry will begin where our life together begins—when we gather for worship. Regular worship together is the heartbeat of ministry, giving life and strength to our day-to-day efforts to respond to God's call. Said another way, the various groups supporting ministry in a Christian community are as spokes on a wheel; coming together for corporate worship brings us to the hub.

The whole body is fitted and joined together, every joint adding its own strength. —Eph. 4:16 (JB)

NINE

Accountability for Ministries

*Brothers and sisters, be all the more eager to confirm your call
and election. –2 Pet. 1:10*

In the parable of the talents, Jesus tells us that we
are accountable for what we do with our gifts and
our time. To be accountable means to answer to
someone who cares about what we do and how we
do it—someone who has an investment in our work.
To be accountable for ministry means answering to
those who invest in our ministry. Wise ministers—lay
or ordained—encourage accountability, for without
it, they have no community of support. Thus, the
minister and support group must be responsible to one
another, to the community that sustains them, and,
ultimately, to God.

The ministry support group does not exist to provide
the minister with a warm, pleasant group of friends

within the church. Rather, the group comes together to help a person follow a particular way of living out the gospel. Like support, accountability has several dimensions, of which the spiritual is the most important and the most easily overlooked. We are accountable not only for doing our ministry but also for the spirit in which we do it. If our ministry becomes disconnected from our prayer life, if we cease to see Christ in the people to whom or with whom we minister, if we no longer do the work of our ministry with joy and love and to God's glory, we may have lost touch with our call.

Changes in the spirit with which we do our ministry are subtle; they may be difficult for us to notice and for those around us to notice—and, once noticed, perhaps even more difficult to talk about. For this reason, it is not easy to provide accountability without a close and continuing support group or relationship within the community of faith. Thus, in discernment, in support, in ministry, we need to work together to help one another in our common journey. We are companions on the way, not adversaries. Faithfulness to our callings demands that we be honest and responsible with each other, to keep from veering aside into dead ends and to remind one another in whose name we travel.

As weighty as the idea of accountability can be, we need not be intimidated by it. Accountability builds relationships of healthy interdependence. Support and accountability are closely intertwined, each being an integral part of the other. If we are not accountable to others for our ministry, especially for its spiritual dimension, how can they support us? If we cannot rely on their support, how can we find the courage to be accountable?

A word of caution is in order. The positive sense of call that the minister feels can lead to the dangerous attitude that the minister is accountable to God alone and need not pay attention to the reservations and concerns of those providing support. Conversely, the positive sense of "ownership" that the support group develops for the minister and vocation can turn into the dangerous notion that the minister is accountable only to that support group. Be wary of either attitude.

A healthy Christian community will encourage its members to become aware of one another and accountable to one another. We need to do every- thing possible to fill the community with an attitude of concern for one another. The genuine call of any person in a Christian community is rightly the concern of all—and a shared responsibility.

> *. . . they called the church together and related all*
> *that God had done with them. . . . –Acts 14:27*

Epilogue: Hearts to Listen

"Live the questions," urges Rainer Maria Rilke. "Perhaps then, someday far in the future, you will gradually, without even noticing it, live your way into the answer."[1]

How can we hear God's call? What could hearing it mean as we live day to day? How can we help each other hear God's voice and follow where God leads? In the end, the questions that open this book cannot be answered by any book. Rather, answers emerge within our hearts as we live the questions. Understanding that God calls us to ministry, preparing our hearts and minds to discern God's call, and meeting with others for insight and support helps us to live these questions. Thus we gain hearts to listen and respond to God's call.

Appendices of
Practical
Suggestions

Appendix 1
Guidelines for Discernment Groups

A discernment group works best if those serving as discerners are trained in prayerful listening, are familiar with varied approaches to meditation, understand the concept of spiritual consensus, and are alert to signs of God's call. Listening Hearts Ministries offers programs that prepare leaders to train discernment teams. For information, see the Listening Hearts web site www.listeninghearts.org, e-mail listening@verizon.net, or call the Listening Hearts office at 410-366-1851.

How To Get Started

To set up the program, a congregation, judicatory, school, or ecumenical group designates an organizer, selects the discerners, and arranges for their training. When the training is completed and the program has been publicized, a contact person assumes responsibility for administering the discernment groups. Every aspect of a request for discernment must be treated with utmost confidentiality.

The goal of the following procedures is to create conditions conducive to hearing God's call. Members of the group gather together, not for discussion or dialogue, but for prayer. The prayer is in silence, in listening, in waiting for the Lord to speak through us. The intent is not decision-making, but to walk with the Lord while living the question. The way is not through counseling techniques, advice, or commentary, but through prayerful, simple questions asked only after quiet reflection. These guidelines can help persons who assimilate them and abide by them to work effectively in discernment groups.[1]

PRIOR TO THE FIRST DISCERNMENT SESSION

1. A person who wishes to explore an issue or a sense of call notifies the contact person.

2. If at all feasible, the contact person meets with that person (the potential focus person[2]) to explain how a discernment group works and to make sure that this is what the person is seeking. If an in-person meeting is not realistic, a phone conversation is a possibility. If the person chooses to continue, the contact person gives the focus person a copy of *Listening Hearts* to read (at least the first seven chapters and Appendices 1 and 2).

3. The contact person, in consultation with the focus person, arranges for a group of three persons from the pool of trained discerners, designating one of them to be the convener.

4. The convener sets up the meeting, consulting with the focus person to choose a comfortable location with a maximum of privacy and freedom from interruption.

5. Three hours should be set aside for each meeting to ensure that those present will not have to leave prematurely. On occasion, the group will not need to use the whole time, but in most cases, it is fruitful to make use of the full three hours.

6. In preparation for the first meeting, the focus person writes a brief sketch not more than one typed page or three pages handwritten. It should begin with a single prayerfully formulated, open-ended question addressed to God. If you are the focus person, avoid multiple choice and "yes or no" questions that limit the directions you are open to moving with the Spirit. Trace significant threads of background and experience that relate to the situation. Then give three copies of the write-up to the convener to distribute to the discerners or e-mail a copy for distribution.

7. The convener distributes a copy of the sketch to each of the other two discerners at least a few days before the meeting. Before the group convenes, members of the group will read the sketch and keep the focus person and the other discerners in their prayers. Praying in preparation for the meeting is extremely important.

8. It takes a long time to assimilate the information in this book. Discerners would be well advised to review Chapters 1 through 7 and Appendices 1 and 2 in preparation for each discernment session. Since the intent of discernment is to develop a clear sense

of what God may be saying, it is particularly important to study Chapter 5, "Is It God We Are Hearing?"

9. It is advisable for the group always to meet as a whole, including the focus person. Thus, it is not recommended that the group of discerners meet among themselves before meeting with the focus person, nor that any discussions take place outside the presence of the focus person.

If any member is unable to attend, the meeting should be rescheduled as soon as possible. In the case of a very long-term discernment issue, if one member of the group needs to withdraw permanently from the commitment, the group may choose to replace that person and have a special meeting to bring the new member up to date.

10. Everyone should come to meetings prepared to schedule a time for another meeting. Those who use appointment calendars should bring them.

At the First Discernment Session

1. The convener arrives at the meeting place well before the starting time to arrange the chairs in an intimate circle, close enough for ease of listening and preferably equidistant from each other with each person able to see the others. As host, it is a good idea for the convener to stand to greet the focus person upon arrival. Some words of welcome to everyone are appropriate when all have gathered.

2. When the group assembles, if all do not know one another, they take some time to introduce themselves with a few words that might be helpful.

3. The convener opens the meeting with some words to help the focus person relax, then possibly a suitable excerpt from Scripture to set the tone. Next, the convener offers an opening prayer, perhaps the Thomas Merton prayer on page 167 of Listening Hearts. Then the convener announces a specified period of silence, perhaps five or ten minutes, to permit all to become receptive to God's presence. At this time, the group may choose to dim the lights to create a more prayerful, reflective atmosphere.

4. The convener ends the silence by having the focus person say, in his or her own words, the issue or question of call, along with a short summary of background information.

5. The task of the members of the group is to listen prayerfully and raise questions that will help the focus person consider the issue. The questions need to be caring and probing, designed to help the person move toward a sense of clearness and a deeper comprehension of the issue in relation to God's call.

6. If the issue being considered is unclear, the first questions must deal with that. If the focus person presents multiple questions or issues, ask the focus person to identify a single question so that all discerners can concentrate on the same question. The other questions may fall away while that question is being addressed, or it may be necessary to consider the questions one at a time. Next, questions to establish relevant background may be in order. The first questions deal with

basic information: circumstances of the situation, the cast of characters, the context. Next, options can be identified and weighed, then known impediments to implementing them. Then the pace of questions slows. The questions become more reflective. More silence is left between the focus person's response and the next question. Slowly, the reflective questions become more evocative, opening up the imagination.

7. Questions should be concise and presented one at a time. Avoid explaining the reason for the question. If you are unsure exactly how to phrase the question, it is better to wait silently to let the question develop and come into clearer focus.

8. The background information supplied by the focus person is often fertile soil for questions. How a person has experienced the Lord's call in the past can be a guide to hearing the Lord now. What is "between the lines" is often as important as what is written; careful, caring inquiry can draw out the unsaid.

9. Avoid questions such as "What does God want you to do?" If the person knew the answer, the group would not be gathered for discernment.

10. Ultimately, the purpose of the questions is to elicit signs of God's call. For this reason, imaginative, intuitive questions can be helpful, even though they may seem "off the wall."

11. Questions designed to call forth Scripture passages and images often bear rich fruit.

12. Members must refrain from giving advice. Do not ask questions that suggest the answer or cloak advice in the guise of questions. Do not ask questions that stem from curiosity alone.

13. It is advisable for the focus person to keep the responses brief because more questions and more silence may provide further clarity. A certain amount of wandering can lead to helpful discoveries; yet if the focus person strays too far off course or keeps repeating things, someone in the group may need to intervene.

14. While articulating answers to the questions is usually helpful, the focus person is never obligated to answer any question. If a question is truly from God, it may plant itself deep within until the focus person is ready to ponder it at some later time.

15. The work of God often takes place in the depth of quiet. It is important that each person be conscious of permitting a period of prayerful silence between speakers.

16. Each member of the group needs to help maintain a pace that allows reflection. Any member of the group, including the focus person, can ask that the cadence of questions slow down or that questions stop altogether for a few minutes of silence.

17. Each member of the group needs to help maintain a gentle atmosphere, guarding against any tendency to become confrontational. This does not mean to avoid asking hard questions. Confrontational questions arise when the questioner wants a given answer or presumes to know what is best for the person. Such questions tend to be expressed with feelings of anger. A good discerner raises questions with a humble and listening heart but is willing to ask difficult questions.

18. Avoid formulating questions in your mind while someone is speaking. Let your questions

develop during the silence between questions. If you need more time to let your question congeal, you may request a period of silence. An atmosphere of open listening must be maintained. It is hard to truly listen to one another.

19. Each member of the group must help ensure that members do not press their own agendas or feelings on the focus person. A discernment session is not about solving a problem. It is an occasion to (1) discover signs of the Spirit in the person's past that led up to the matter being considered, (2) see what God might be trying to say through the present situation, and (3) develop a sense of where the Spirit might be pointing.

20. Each member of the group should try to make sure that others in the group have the opportunity to speak.

21. During the meeting, members of the group can test whether they are really listening to one another by keeping in mind these two questions: Do I have an open mind with respect to the issues being considered? Is anything keeping me from really listening to one of the persons present?

22. The session usually takes the entire three hours, in which case a break is recommended. The group can determine whether the break will be silent or talking. Following the break it is usually helpful to take a few minutes of silence to become centered once again, after which the convener can invite the group to pick up where it left off.

23. In the course of a discernment session, various threads emerge. Toward the end of the session, it is helpful to raise questions that help draw these threads together.

24. About thirty minutes before the anticipated end of the meeting, the convener begins to look for an opening to reverse gears by offering the focus person an opportunity to ask something of the group. Perhaps the focus person will want silence or to hear experiences the discerners have had that offer parallels. It is the time for the focus person to do the asking and for the group to respond.

On occasion a focus person has asked that each member of the group take a turn inviting a prayer image. To do this, each discerner, one at a time, stands behind the focus person with hands on the head of the focus person. In silence and with eyes closed, the discerner holds the focus person in prayer, awaiting a "picture" that may bring insight to the unfolding situation. The discerner describes the image in as much detail as possible without offering an interpretation. This exercise has produced some vivid perceptions. Any discerner for whom a picture does not arise may offer a prayer or simply say "amen."

25. About ten minutes before the end of the meeting, the convener asks the group to determine whether or not another meeting is desirable. If anyone in the group is not fully at peace with the direction in which the focus person seems to be moving, it is exceedingly important for that person to suggest that the group convene again. Everyone needs to keep in mind the importance of spiritual consensus in this process. Anyone in the group should feel free to raise a question to check the sense of the group.

Sometimes another meeting is useful, if only to give the focus person and the group time to reflect and pray. If another meeting is not planned, the group should make it clear that the focus person can request another meeting at a later time by contacting the convener.

26. The final five minutes are for free and open prayers, which the convener introduces and concludes.

27. At any time during the meeting, a sense that the group has crossed a threshold may emerge. A member may suggest that a common understanding seems to exist. Should this occur, the convener may check out this perception with the group and, if verified, begin to conclude the meeting as suggested in guideline 24.

28. Discernment sessions are occasions for quickening; much of what transpires occurs at a later time. A meeting or series of meetings can take place without resolution of the issue raised by the focus person. The consensus may be that the group has gone as far as it can for the time being. Should this occur, the desire to "wrap things up" neatly or to come to closure on a particular question should be resisted. Later events, choices, or circumstances may become the place where God brings to fruition the work that has been done. Neither the planting nor the harvest belongs to us. Thus, at the time the meetings conclude, it is wise to avoid summary advice or comment so that we do not reap before the time of the harvest.

29. It is essential that what goes on in the meeting be absolutely confidential unless the focus person expressly chooses otherwise. If the focus person wants to initiate talk with a member of the group at a future date, that is permissible. No discerner should ever initiate any discussion of the subject with anyone outside of the meeting except at the focus person's request.

30. At the conclusion of the final session with a given focus person, all discerners should return their copies of the introductory sketch to the focus person.

AFTER THE MEETING

1. Prayer and discernment continue after the group disperses. Any member of the group may subsequently develop a strong sense that it would be beneficial to reconvene, in which case that person may call the convener and suggest another meeting. The convener would then call the focus person to see if the focus person would like the group to come back together again. And of course, the focus person is always at liberty to initiate the group's gathering again by notifying the convener.

2. On the rare occasion that discerners may encounter a serious problem in terms of how they dealt with a discernment session, they may need to meet without the focus person to address their own handling of the situation. At such a meeting, it is crucial that the discerners discuss procedures only and make no reference to the content of the discernment issue. It is also important that they do

nothing to cast blame on the focus person, but look only at how they might have worked together more constructively.

REMINDERS FOR DISCERNERS

• Remember that first and foremost you are gathered for prayer. Try to be attuned to one another and to the Holy Spirit so that your group is unified, truly the body of Christ present in that place.

• Discernment is a fluid process. The focus person comes with a question based on one or more concerns. Quite often, the question evolves and the initial problems recede. Try to make sure that the original issue has truly been resolved. Otherwise, the focus person may leave feeling serene but wake up the next morning experiencing the turmoil of the problem anew.

• Even if the issue appears simple, do not assume that only one discernment session will be required for the person. Beneath a simple issue may be a more complex question. Arriving at the real focus question is an important aspect of discernment.

• Avoid functioning as three individuals charting separate paths. Instead, try to become attuned to the Holy Spirit flowing through one another so that you can be drawn forward as one body. Build on the questions of others. Listen to the focus person's responses and ask follow-up questions.

• Try to not simply follow where the focus person leads. Continually remind yourself that you are following the Holy Spirit. Likewise, a discerner with a strong personality may become the leader. Slow down to re-establish the Holy Spirit as the leader.

• Do not store up your questions. Listen, listen, listen. Let the Holy Spirit determine if and when the opportunity comes to raise the questions that occur to you. If you lose a thought, trust the Spirit to return it to you if the question is from God, or that someone else will ask it. This kind of prayerful listening will prevent jumping prematurely from one line of questions to another.

• In a discernment session, a focus person sometimes becomes strongly drawn to one particular thing: a Scripture passage, a dream, a memory, an analogy, certain words, a particular question, or a visual image. This may be a key to unlock a door. If the discerners explore and probe possible associations, the right questions may arise, and the door may open.

• When you detect energy in a person's response, take note and look for follow-up questions.

• Sometimes a person feels a strong sense of call but does not seem to be able to follow the call. This person may seek discernment to find out what stands in the way of living out that call. In such a situation, it may be important to consider the possibility that the call may be authentic, but some aspect of the call may not be properly understood. A genuine call usually produces the energy to fulfill it.

• On the one hand, discernment needs to be expansive and imaginative, opening up the doors to possibilities beyond our desires or expectations. On the other hand, discerners must stay in touch with the practical realities of the situation. In the course of any session, it is advisable to explore both ends of the spectrum.

• Encapsulate the focus person's responses in silence. If the focus person's response goes unusually deep or strikes a profound emotional chord, leave extra time for the impact to penetrate before raising another question. Imagine the reverberation of a temple bell as it trails off slowly into the distance. The more intense the gong, the longer the reverberation. Likewise, the deeper the question and response go, the stronger the impact and the more time it takes to absorb it.

• If the group seems to be grasping for questions, it probably indicates that the questions are coming from the head. This is a good time for someone to ask for a period of silence so that the group can become more centered and unified, more confident that God will provide. The best discernment questions usually quietly bubble up from deep down. It is the quality of the questions, not the quantity or frequency, that brings forth spiritual discernment.

• Refrain from asking questions that imply an accusation. Wait until you can present the question in a more neutral way.

• Avoid asking questions that presuppose a statement that the focus person has not made. For example, do not ask, "Why are you angry with your mother?" if the person has not articulated that she is angry with her mother. Instead, pose an evocative question such as, "If you try to feel your mother's presence, what colors come to mind?" or "What kind of music do you hear?"

• Be mindful of signs of the Spirit. It is important to distinguish between pleasant feelings of serenity and the peace of God, which presents itself as a strong sense of confidence and well-being arising from deep within—often welling up from beneath the turbulence of a difficult situation. It is crucial that each member of the group share a true sense of God's peace. Any member who feels any sense of agitation or disquiet needs to make it known so that the discernment can continue until the peace of God envelops the entire gathering, bringing forth true spiritual consensus.

- If the focus person is emotionally fragile because of a recent crisis or personal loss, sound judgment may dictate that it is not an appropriate time to raise hard questions. In such a case, when the convener asks if anyone thinks another meeting would be useful, someone can say something such as, "I think that we have gone as far as we can for the moment. Perhaps we should let matters rest and get together again in six months or so."

- If the focus person has serious emotional problems, the group should not press too far. In this type of situation, when the convener asks if another meeting is needed, someone might say that the matter is not really resolved, but that the group has gone as far as it can so there is probably no need to schedule another meeting.

- In the final segment of the meeting, if the focus person asks the members of the group to share their own experiences, do not present your experience in a way that gives advice. Your experience can speak for itself; the focus person can glean from it what is helpful. Limit your response to what the focus person has asked of you.

Appendix 2
Types of Questions to Raise When Serving in Discernment Groups

The words *question* and *quest* come from the same Latin root, *quaerere*, which means "to search or seek." This is the context in which we use questions for discernment: not to interrogate but to explore—looking for signs that point the way for us. Thomas Merton offered testimony to the value of well-conceived questions when he wrote the following of his professor at Columbia, Mark Van Doren:

> Most of the time he asked questions. His questions were very good, and if you tried to answer them intelligently, you found yourself saying things that you did not know you knew, and that you had not, in fact, known before. He had "educed" them from you by his question. Do not think that Mark was simply priming his students with thoughts of his own, and then making the thought stick to their minds by getting them to give it back to him as their own. . . . The results were sometimes quite unexpected . . . casting lights that he had not himself foreseen.[1]

Discernment questions are like this. They help us to become conscious of what we know deep within but have never been able to articulate. More importantly, they can open us up to the presence of the Spirit or raise our awareness of the absence of the Spirit.

In order to develop discernment-type questions, we need to have a foundation of information firmly in place. For this reason, the initial questions must be informational in intent. This first segment of questions might take only a few minutes or could take much longer, depending on the circumstances. During this time, it can be helpful if discerners keep the following points in mind:

1. If the focus question is unclear or ambiguous, the very first questions should help the focus person sharpen that question.

2. If the issue before the group contains more than one question, ask the focus person to identify the primary question so that everyone can concentrate on a single question. As that question gets resolved, the others may fall into place. If this does not happen, the group can address a second question after it has gone as far as it can with the first one.

3. Once the focus question is clearly established, the next questions are for the purpose of clarifying or fleshing out background information. If anything in the focus person's write-up or presentation needs elaboration, this is the time to ask for it.

4. If anyone in the group does not know the focus person reasonably well, it is useful to learn something of the focus person's interests (family, job, pastimes,

hobbies). This information can serve as soil for imaginative questions later.

5. Before proceeding to questions that are more explicitly aimed at discernment, it may help to ask about things such as:

- What options exist
- The advantages and disadvantages of various courses of action
- Risks and cost involved
- What impact any decision will have on other people (family, colleagues, competitors)
- The thoughts and feelings of other people who may be affected
- The focus person's abilities, strengths, and weaknesses
- Any commitments that might be compromised
- Practical considerations
- Whether the person is overworked, too busy, or not busy enough

DISCERNMENT QUESTIONS

Once the information is clear and adequate, the pace of the questions needs to slow down so that each question and response is encased in silence. It can be useful to take some time for silence to provide a transition into this portion of the session, which is a time of prayerful, centered listening.

Discernment questions do not come from the top of the head. Rather, they come through one's spiritual heart (the gut). They come from the Spirit, activated as the group sits united in prayer—listening and waiting with open hearts and minds.

Some discernment questions are reflective in nature. They help the focus person to: (a) reflect on his or her motives, (b) get in touch with desires and fears, (c) explore when and how God has worked in his or her life over the years, and (d) notice where and how God has been acting in relation to the specific issue under consideration.

Other discernment questions are evocative. Such questions help a person uncover thoughts and feelings that are below the surface. Emotions can be very complex. When you ask people how they feel, usually they can mention only the emotions that are closest to the surface. It is better to help them find metaphors that can uncover a wide range of feelings and thoughts. For this purpose, evocative questions that call forth images tend to be more fruitful than overt questions. Analogies sparked by drawing upon a person's areas of interest (sports, business, finance, family, nature) can be explored to reveal signs of God's presence. The group can invite associations with Scripture, art, music, literature, or science as a way of bringing signs of the Spirit to light.

It is preferable for discerners to help the focus person access his or her own images as opposed to suggesting those that come to them. As a discerner, whenever possible, try to let the ideas and images that come to you increase your own understanding, which in turn can help you pose questions that enable the focus person to hit upon his or her own analogies, metaphors, or Scripture references.

As we try to help others find their sense of direction, we do not want to directly use a list of questions. The list below is to stimulate, to suggest kinds of questions that can be helpful. It may be useful to read them over in advance before gathering for discernment and then put the list aside.

Three areas of questions are suggested: questions to the person seeking discernment; questions for members of the group to consider while listening to the person seeking discernment; and supplemental questions to people considering ordained ministry.

QUESTIONS TO THE PERSON SEEKING DISCERNMENT

• Is this something you have thought about doing for a long time? Is now the time? How do you know?

• Are you feeling rushed to make a decision? Do you feel in a hurry to get on with it?

• What people have influenced your thinking on this matter?

• What are your impulses? instincts? inclinations? What are their sources?

• Do you feel obligated to do this? Do you feel that it is your duty? Is this expected of you?

• Will you resent doing this?

• Does your kindness and affability make you vulnerable to manipulation by people?

• Is a desire to be loved influencing you? Might a desire for approval be influencing you?

• How concerned are you about your reputation?

- Is money a factor in your decision?
- What are the needs of the community? What do those needs suggest to you?
- Are you trying to be obedient to God? What if God says no?
- Are any stories from your life related to this issue? What are they?
- A person considering whether to continue a ministry (for example, working at a shelter for the homeless) may be asked to consider these questions: Do I see Christ in the people involved? Do they see Christ in me? Will a new direction help me reflect Christ in a better way?
- As you think about your situation, is there a person in the Bible with whom you identify?
- Does any theme or passage from Scripture occur to you as you wrestle with this?
- What colors would you select to express your feelings at this moment?
- *If the focus person is interested in sports:* How do athletes approach this kind of challenge? *or* Can you draw an analogy with any athletic endeavor?
- *To a person who is an avid reader:* Do you feel like a character in any book you have read?
- *To a person who is interested in the theater:* Does any play come to mind as you consider this issue?
- *To a music lover:* As you envision taking that path, what kind of music do you hear playing?
- *To a weaver or a person who enjoys sewing:* Can you describe the fabric that might convey this situation?
- *If the focus person speaks of running into a wall:* What is the wall made of? How high is it? How thick?

(Then explore the properties of whatever materials constitute the wall.) How might you go over, through, or around it? Does any Scripture passage speak to you about this? What is on the other side?

• *If the focus person makes reference to a door:* Is the door open or closed? What happens if you step through the door? What do you see? Can you smell anything? What does it feel like in there? What happens if you do not go through?

• *If the focus person makes reference to a road:* Do you recognize this road? Are you alone on the road? What does it look like? Is it dark or light out? Are you walking? Driving? Can you see what is ahead? What is on either side? Are you comfortable on this road? Do you wish to get off it? If so, do you see an exit? Is it open or blocked?

QUESTIONS FOR MEMBERS OF THE DISCERNMENT GROUP TO CONSIDER

• Has the person told us everything? Are there gaps or inconsistencies in what the person has told us? Is the body language consistent with what is being said? How can we best elicit the unsaid?

• Is the person's perception of a call limited because of social background, role, and stereotype? How can we explore this issue? How can we help expand the horizons?

• Are the discerners working together to follow the movement of the Spirit in exploring themes and images?

• Is there a need for more extended silence? (Remember that whoever requests the silence concludes the silence so that further questions may come forth.)

• As the focus person speaks, are themes or threads recurring that can be brought together toward the end of the discernment session?

SUPPLEMENTAL QUESTIONS FOR PEOPLE SEEKING DISCERNMENT OF CALL TO ORDAINED MINISTRY

• How do you envision your ministry? What do you sense is the work you are being called to do?

• What events and circumstances have led you toward considering a call to ordained ministry?

• Can you perform your ministry without being ordained? If not, why not?

• Do you see pastoral care as central to your ministry?

• Do you think of yourself as a "servant"?

• Are your abilities commensurate with the demands of ordained ministry? What are your strengths? What are your weaknesses?

• How are you perceived by others?

• Do the people in your congregation experience you as a leader within their community? How do you know?

• To what extent does your sense of call come through your faith community? How strong is your sense of the church as community?

• To what extent would your ordination impact your family?

- What debts do you have? Is seminary financially feasible for you? How would you finance your seminary education? Could the debt you might incur affect your ability to carry out God's call once ordained? What if you became ordained and could not find a paid position in the church?
- Are you aware of the criticism and rejection an ordained minister often receives? Could you handle this? How?
- Are you aware of the adulation an ordained minister often receives? How would you handle this?
- How do you feel about the authority of the church hierarchy?
- What weight do you give to the authority of the people of a congregation?
- How does Scripture impact your life?
- How does Scripture direct your ministry?

All involved in discerning a call to an ordained ministry need to become fully familiar with all of the pertinent guidelines and publications issued by their respective denomination. Such documents will generate their own questions.

When discerning what may be a call to ordination, it is particularly important that the group await a strong and clear consensus to confirm that the call is perceived by both the candidate and the corporate body. Remember that spiritual discernment is marked by signs of God's Spirit evident among those taking part in the discernment.

Since genuine discernment depends on a willing and open heart, mandating discernment could violate its nature. Therefore making discernment groups available for aspirants is preferable to requiring the use of such groups. Furthermore, because strict confidentiality is a crucial condition for honest sharing, a discernment group cannot be expected to issue a report other than to state that the discernment has taken place and concluded that the person is being called to continue exploring a possible call to a particular ministry. Any additional communication must necessarily come from the candidate.

Screening is best seen as a separate and complementary endeavor, with each informing the other.

SUMMARY FOR SEQUENCE OF QUESTIONS FOR DISCERNMENT SESSIONS

Step 1

Make sure that the discernment question is clear.

Step 2

Develop a good grasp of the basic information: circumstances of the situation, the cast of characters, the context.

Step 3

Identify options, weigh them, find out known impediments to implementing them. If you have "What would you do?", "What might you say?" kinds of questions, ask them here. Some reflective questions fit in this segment.

Step 4

When the first steps have been fulfilled, move on to pose the deeper kinds of reflective questions and evocative questions. Try not to revert to the informational questions that belong in steps 1, 2, and 3. Toward the end of this section, begin to raise questions that help connect the various strands that have emerged in the course of the discernment to integrate them.

If a discerner sees the group moving to the next step before he or she feels fully ready, that discerner should request a period of silence to provide time to sit quietly with what has been developing.

Appendix 3
Informal History of the Project and the Research Methods Used

by Suzanne Farnham

The ideas that eventually developed into this book began to percolate in April 1987 at Kirkridge Retreat and Study Center in Bangor, Pennsylvania, at a conference, "Solitude and Community." Parker Palmer, one of the conference leaders, spoke at length about the Quakers and set up small groups to meet in the evenings and function as Quaker "clearness committees." In a Friends Meeting, a person who is wrestling with a personal decision can ask for a clearness committee—a small group of people to meet with and help the person develop a sense of direction.

As one who has constantly wrestled with personal questions of vocation, I volunteered to be a "focus person." Parker distributed some guidelines. We dived in. Most of the people at the conference were Protestant clergy with backgrounds strong in pastoral counseling and weak in contemplation. They found it difficult to abide by guidelines requiring Quaker silence and not giving advice. Even so, the process proved helpful, and I experienced an increased sense of clarity. It seemed to be a method worth taking back to my parish.

At the same conference, I struck up a conversation with Jan Hoffman, who, at that time, was Clerk of the New England Yearly Meeting of Friends. When she heard I was from Baltimore, she mentioned that the Baltimore Friends were known and respected nationwide. I had not known this and began to think it would be good to capitalize on such a resource.

Upon returning home, I began to consider making a little study: reading a few books, interviewing a few Quakers, and attending some Friends Meetings.

Things soon began to snowball. I started to feel that the Quakers had a highly effective process but did not sufficiently use some of the tests of discernment employed by others. My thought was to integrate the two.

For several years I had been looking for a concise compilation of principles for discernment that went beyond the Ignatian Rules, but to no avail. My spiritual director, Patricia Scanlan, then prioress of the Baltimore Carmel, suggested that all of the spiritual classics were laced with information on discernment of call, although not necessarily using those terms. With help from Mother Virginia of the All Saints Convent, Barbara Platt, who is theologically trained and at the time served as executive director of the Stoney Run Friends in Baltimore, and Bill Rich, who then headed the deacons' formation program for the Diocese of

Maryland, I put together a bibliography. The list was too long for me to handle alone, so I began to recruit people to help with the reading. The vestry of Memorial Church pledged to support the work. The Committee on the Ministry of the Laity of the Diocese of Maryland gave $500 to purchase the books. Bishop Eastman provided a grant for new initiatives. The Christian Vocation Research Project was under way.

I bought books, purchased hi-liters and colored pens, and made out an instruction sheet. Each volunteer was to read an assigned book, marking the portions of the book containing information on call, discernment, or community according to a color-coded scheme. They were also invited to make comments in the margins and to write summaries when the material was implicit or diffuse. It took forty people to do this reading, which included over one hundred titles.

Another problem arose: the amount of information gathered was overwhelming. As a solution, I recruited five of the readers to help sift through the material, organize and evaluate it, design a discernment program for use in parishes, and put together a handbook. Naively, I said that we would meet for an hour and a half every week for three months. In fact, we met almost every week for over two years; some of the meetings lasted all day.

One of the five, Andy Barasda, was between jobs and had offered to help us get started but had said that he might not be able to continue for the full three months. He put in five months before retiring.

A second member of the group, Jenny Ramberg, met with us weekly for the first nine months. Her sudden and untimely death dealt a big loss because of her personal warmth as well as her scholarship in feminist theology. This left us with the group of four— Joe, Teto, Sue, and me—who met weekly for another year and a half and eventually came to realize that we were writing a book, not just a handbook.

Before the original group of six met, Joe volunteered to take notes of the meetings, enter them on his computer, and print and distribute them to the group for review and reflection. This offer turned out to be crucial to the development of the project. After our very first meeting, I realized that it was going to be very difficult to keep track of all the data. I asked Joe if he could extract the pieces of information from the minutes and catalog them according to category. He asked me to come up with subdivisions. I identified eight questions that we were trying to answer; these became the titles for our eight working papers. From that point on, as each of us went through the books that had been read and marked, we wrote down relevant information, indicating which working paper it was to go on, and gave it to Joe. Every entry was numbered and entered as a separate item on one of the eight working papers. Since these papers were fluid, we dated each edition. These were the foundation for our work when we gathered.

Every meeting began with ten minutes of silence. When the need for further silence arose in the course of a meeting, we either fell into it naturally or someone requested it. We worked through all of the information using spiritual consensus. Each idea from the working papers was considered until every-one agreed what to do with it: integrate it into a preliminary draft that we called a "narrative," include it in a note, or drop it. The titles of the narratives corresponded to the titles of the working papers. Joe worked our decisions into the narratives—not a small task! Then, as the narratives were refined, they became drafts of chapters 1 through 7 or appendices 1 and 2.

The following sample from one page of one working paper from a specific date helps to illustrate the process:

How Can We Evaluate If
It Is God We Are Hearing?

Where to Look

54. "In order to discern we need to learn how to read our own history, to see the turning points, the movements of change, the unfolding of God's plan for us at each new step of the way." (de Waal, p. 73.)

56. Christ addresses me in the voice of each person I meet. (de Waal, p. 126.)

63. Discover what you believe and value by observing what you do. (Kelsey & Haldane.)

64. Examine your ideas against the opposite ideas.

66. Some thoughts come through direct inspiration, some through God's friends, some through creatures or objects.

85. When trying to tap the full potential of any nucleus of human energy, you need to tap into those qualities within it which are unique and incommunicable. (de Chardin, *Building the Earth.*)

104. John the Baptist's disciples complained to him that the people were now being baptized by Jesus, the person to whom John had bore witness. John replied,

"A person can lay claim only to what is given him from heaven."

115. The poor are too often left to God. Therefore, forget those who are better placed and remember the poor. (Fox/Eckhart.)

121. There are stories from our lives through which God is trying to tell us things we need to know. We need to identify those stories, tell them, and try to sort them out. (Multiple sources.)

124. Discover what you believe and value by observing what you do. (Multiple sources.)

128. What the god does is more important than the words people say. (Egyptian Book of Amen, as related in *Proclamation Commentaries: Genesis, Exodus, Leviticus, Numbers*, Foster R. McCurley, Ed.)

Some entries were rearranged, so that the numbers were not necessarily in sequence. As entries were processed and integrated into the narratives, they dropped out of the working papers.

In preparation for each meeting, members of the group handed in new entries, Joe updated the working papers and narratives and eventually the chapters we would be using, and I made copies and distributed them to the others ahead of time.

At the same time, a separate area of inquiry was also under way. In the early stages of thinking about this project, Fred Wolf, who was then Bishop of Maine, suggested that it was important that any work on discernment of call address the issues of support for ministry and accountability. To investigate these areas of concern, another group of people set about gathering information. Each person took responsibility for studying a different group: the Quakers, the Lutherans, the Episcopal Diocese of Central New York, the rural parishes in the Episcopal Diocese of Delaware, the Sojourners, the Church of the Saviour in Washington, D.C., and the Kittamaqundi Community in Columbia, Maryland. They interviewed people, made visitations, did reading and then synthesized their findings by coming together for discussion on three Saturdays. Those who saw this portion of the research effort through to completion were Barbara Cates, Jeff Eller, Barney Farnham, Pam Fleming, Caroline Naylor, and Dick Roszel. The fruits of this research became chapters 8 and 9.

The copy editor, authors, and theologians who read through the various drafts of the manuscript and made suggestions became our teachers, our mentors.

As the guidelines for discernment took shape, we developed a training program for discerners. We field-tested the book, the training program, and the discernment group, all with the help of our consultant, Russell Ayers.

We then incorporated as a nonprofit organization for the purpose of implementing our programs and continuing the research. The bylaws of the corporation stipulate that all meetings of the trustees and of any committees be conducted incorporating silence and arriving at decisions through spiritual consensus.

Writing this book was itself an experience in Christian community that touched our lives deeply.

Appendix 4
Listening Hearts Program Opportunities

You can read about a foreign country and thereby get an introduction to life in that place and a foundation for understanding its culture. After that, a visit can give you a bit of a feel for that culture. But to assimilate the culture, you have to move there and live among its people for a period of time.

Spiritual discernment runs counter to the culture in which we live. Reading about discernment is an important first step in learning about it. But to internalize the culture of spiritual discernment, you have to spend time in it. Listening Hearts programs offer the opportunity to experience this culture. An hour and a half workshop can get your toes wet. Programs that take several days provide an immersion experience. The ultimate goal is to cultivate a life of discernment.

Because a community of support is important to developing and maintaining the practice of discernment, Listening Hearts programs are offered primarily to communities of faith such as congregations, seeker groups, governing boards, clergy groups, schools, and dioceses/judicatories. Each program is held at a location chosen by the sponsoring group.

Retreats and workshops afford a setting and structure for participants to engage in spiritual discernment around their own life situations. Silence, solitude, Scripture, song, creative meditation activities, and communal sharing weave together to draw people closer to God and each other as they gain direction for their lives.

1. *Listening Hearts Retreats* give members of a group an avenue to seek God's guidance about the personal or professional issues they face and bring them together in a way that builds Christian community. These retreats are suitable for congregations, groups of seekers, student groups, diocesan/judicatory gatherings, clergy groups, or conference center programs. Each retreat is custom designed to meet the needs of the specific group.

2. *Grounded in God Retreats* teach decision-making groups how to work through their issues using reverent speaking, prayerful listening, creative engagement with Scripture, and spiritual consensus. Groups that commit to this approach find that controversial issues can draw members closer to God and one another.

3. An *Eight-Day Spiritual Discernment Retreat* provides an immersion experience in both *Listening Hearts* (discernment in community for individual personal discernment) and *Grounded in God* (discernment for group deliberations). This retreat is particularly appropriate for clergy groups.

4. *Opening the Ear of Your Heart* offers spiritual conflict resolution to congregations, judicatories, governing boards, or any other church group in which members are wrestling with a divisive issue.

Training Programs for Trainers take prospective trainers through the program they will be teaching, supplemented by workshops to learn the procedures and mechanics of how to conduct the training.

1. The *Training Week for Trainers* is an intense six-day event, sponsored by a congregation, diocese, or regional division of a denomination. It takes place at a retreat facility selected by the sponsoring group. Registration is limited to eight people who take their spiritual lives seriously, have leadership ability, and are willing to train groups in Listening Hearts discernment. The training prepares leaders to train groups of up to 10 in a congregation to serve as a discernment ministry team. This team can lead *Listening Hearts* book discussions, conduct adult forum sessions, offer retreat mornings, serve in discernment groups, and encourage the practice of prayerful listening in the congregation or organization. On occasion, an alternative option is offered for people who want the training, but are unable to get an entire group together. The "Plan Two" Training Weeks for Trainers are seven-day programs for a maximum of six participants at a retreat house in Maryland.

2. *Community Discernment for Call to Ministry* is a program that trains trainers for a diocese/judicatory to go into congregations and train groups to serve as discernment groups within their congregations. This program provides the opportunity for any member of a congregation who wants to explore a possible call to ministry, whether in the church or in daily life and whether or not it might require ordination, to ask for a discernment group. This *Training of Trainers*

program entails two forty-eight hour retreats, three weeks apart, that begin at 4 p.m. on Thursday and conclude at 4 p.m. on Saturday. All of the program design sheets, information and instruction sheets, feedback forms, and musical accompaniment needed for the work with congregations are made available to the trainers electronically.

For detailed information about any program, contact the Listening Hearts office at listening@verizon.net or (410) 366-1851, or go to www.listeninghearts.org.

Notes

Introduction

1. Ware, p. 187.
2. Bonhoeffer, *Letters and Papers*, p. 346. "The 'heart' in the Biblical sense is ... the whole [person] in relation to God."
3. Ware, throughout.
4. Kierkegaard, *A Kierkegaard Anthology*, pp. 4–5.

Chapter 1. What Is "Call" for the Christian?

1. **Call** can be used interchangeably with the word **vocation,** which comes from the Latin word **vocare,** "to call." **Vocation,** however, often has a broad connotation, while **call** may refer to something more specific. A person might have a vocation as a choral director, for example, and a call to work with a specific chorus at a particular time.
2. See Luther, p. 311. Luther compares the call of a priest or monk to the call of a farmer laboring in the field or a woman looking after her home. See also de Waal, p. 117. De Waal writes that the Rule of St. Benedict, which sets forth the aims and practices of

the Benedictine monastic life, "totally cuts through the sham that any one person is superior to any other or could have more value than any other."

3. Compare Luther, p. 311.
4. Futrell, **Ignatian Discernment,** p. 49; see also de Waal, p. 153.
5. Futrell, **Ignatian Discernment,** p. 49.
6. de Waal, p. 153. To think of God as outside the places or circumstances of our own life can prevent us from hearing God's call. Buber, p. 74, put it this way:

> Creation is not a hurdle on the road to God; it is the road itself. We are created along with one another and directed to a life with one another. Creatures are placed in my way so that I, their fellow creature, by means of them and with them, may find the way to God. A God reached by excluding them would not be the God of all beings in whom all being is fulfilled.

Buber wrote this in disagreement with Sören Kierkegaard (quoted in Buber, p. 74), who had renounced his relationship with Regina Olsen, saying, "In order to come to love, I had to remove the object."

7. Compare Orsy, pp. 160–61.
8. McNeill, Morrisson, and Nouwen, p. 83. While the authors discuss only the distinction between vocation and career, not everyone has a job that is also a career. Yet there is an equally valid distinction between vocation and occupation, i.e., one's livelihood, whether or not it is a career. Work, of itself, may or may not be vocation. Undue emphasis on work of any kind can leave little time, place, or room for God's call. See de Waal, p. 107: "There is

no nonsense here about it being in some way praise-
worthy to be overworked."

On the other hand, as our lives become more
centered in God, we tend to grow in our sense that
God touches others through our work, whatever that
work may be. When we go into the workplace, we carry
Christ with us. See Brother Lawrence, throughout.

Ordained ministers can be particularly susceptible
to regarding their priestly occupations as synonymous
with God's call. Ordained ministers also have respon-
sibilities toward family, friends, and self. To ignore
such responsiblities and devote time excessively
to matters of ordained ministry can deafen even a
priestly ear to God's entire call. Thus, C. S. Lewis
cautioned Sheldon Vanauken against becoming a
priest because it could debase his Christianity by
turning it into an occupation. Vanauken, pp. 105–6.

9. Compare Burtness, p. 92.

10. "Are we to understand the 'imitation of Christ' in
the sense that we should copy his life," asks Carl G.
Jung, "or in the deeper sense that we are to live our
own proper lives as truly as he lived his in its individual uniqueness?" Jung answers his own question:
"It is no easy matter to live a life that is modelled
on Christ's, but it is unspeakably harder to live one's
own life as truly as Christ lived his." Jung, p. 340.

11. Futrell, *Ignatian Discernment,* p. 54. Compare
Merton, *New Seeds,* p. 32. Merton writes, "Our
vocation is not simply to *be,* but to work together
with God in the creation of our own life, our own
identity, our own destiny." See also Merton, *Seven
Storey Mountain,* p. 130.

12. L'Engle, p. 27.

13. Green, pp. 139–40. Green sees the devil testing us by
false "consolation," an apparent, though mistaken,

feeling of spiritual peace that locks us in place and prevents us from moving forward in greater service to the Lord. Barclay, pp. 267–68, discusses the parable of the wedding feast, pointing out that the things that make people deaf to God's call are not necessarily bad in themselves:

> One man went to his estate, the other to his business. They did not go off on a wild carousal or an immoral adventure. They went off on the, in itself, excellent task of efficiently administering their business life . . . . The tragedy of life is that it is so often the second bests which shut out the bests, that it is things which are good in themselves which shut out the things that are supreme.

14. Compare Green, p. 99: "Discernment is where prayer meets action." See James 2:17: "So faith by itself, if it has no works, is dead." See also de Waal, p. 78: "We get there by deeds, not words."
15. Compare de Waal, p. 17: "Genuine fruitfulness comes from what at first seems sterile."
16. The image of fruit seems particularly apt when describing the results of responding to God's call. It may take many years before a seed becomes a tree. Even after the tree is grown, it may be a long time before it produces fruit and still longer before the fruit ripens. It is a mistake to look for immediate results after responding to God's call. Such a stance can encourage people to manufacture forced or artificial fruit, as if to "prove" a call from God. Nevertheless, it is well for us to consider the possibility that if we do not bear fruit, we may be gathered up and burned (John 15:6).
17. McNeill, Morrison, and Nouwen, p. 36.

18. McNeill, Morrison, and Nouwen, p. 40. See also p. 36: "Obedience is hearing God's loving word and responding to it." Compare de Waal, p. 43: "... to obey really means to hear and then act upon what we have heard."
19. de Waal, p. 49.
20. Servant Leadership School Program Offerings, p. 2.
21. Ulanov and Ulanov, p. 9.

CHAPTER 2. CALL TO MINISTRY

1. Fenhagen, *Mutual Ministry,* p. 21.
2. *The Book of Common Prayer,* p. 855 (from the "Catechism").
3. Compare Sedgwick, p. 6: "... when ministry focuses on the image of service alone then specific acts of service become ends in themselves."
4. Williams, p. 193.

CHAPTER 3. WHAT IS DISCERNMENT?

1. Futrell, *Ignatian Discernment,* p. 47. Futrell discusses the Ignatian concept of *diakrisis pneumaton,* "discernment of Spirits."
2. As with all gifts from God, there is no way to compel the gift of discernment. Compare Green, p. 116: "There are no techniques for producing the experience of God."
3. Diocese of Bethlehem, p. 1.
4. Compare Ignatius of Loyola, pp. 129–34, "Rules for the Discernment of Spirits." Even these rules, which are for perceiving and understanding "to some degree" the different movements produced in the soul, are not so much rules as they are an outline of

peaks (consolations) and valleys (desolations) on a spiritual landscape.

5. Sheeran, pp. 24–25.

6. Sheeran, p. 24.

7. Sheeran, p. 25, quoting Vernon Noble.

8. Sheeran, p. 25. Another test used by the early Quakers was a person's own "inner leadings." Yet as Sheeran points out (pp. 26, 28–29), in assessing those leadings the early Quakers failed to consider the writings on discernment that preceded them, such as those of Ignatius. Nor did they use any external benchmark to test such leadings.

   Compare Johnston, *The Still Point,* p. 114. Johnston discusses G.K. Chesterton's distaste for what Chesterton called "Funny Interior Feeling." Chesterton (quoted in Johnston, p. 114) said, "When Jones obeys the inner light, Jones obeys Jones." Chesterton articulates Roman Catholic thinking from the time of the Reformation, which stresses reliance on external, ecclesiastical authority to guide conduct. Johnston is also wary of reliance on inner feelings alone. He suggests (pp. 114–16) that inner promptings can come from our own neuroses and that, since most people are not sufficiently developed spiritually, "a science of ethics and asceticism is necessary."

9. Futrell, *Ignatian Discernment,* p. 53.

10. The understanding that discernment takes place in a close relationship with the Lord may offer the best insight into how discernment occurs. Thinking of discernment as a process or an art may be helpful but also invites problems.

    Green, p. 57, states that discernment is "the art of finding God's will." This is useful as a contrast to merely applying rules or precepts that may frustrate discernment, but it can also be misleading. The essence of art is individual creativity. While the ability to discern also involves creativity, it occurs, not by individual effort alone, but through a relationship with the Lord. As Green, p. 64, also says:

> The essential truth [is] that discernment is a function of a loving, personal relationship to the Lord. It can normally be only as deep and as solid as that relationship itself. The true discerner must be a praying, loving person.

Another word used to describe how discernment occurs is *process.* This word often strikes a chord with those who have a strong bent for the spiritual because they frequently perceive life, death, and resurrection as a continuing process.

"Process theology" takes the radical viewpoint that all of creation, including God, is dynamic and in the process of change. What is real is in process. Alfred North Whitehead is considered the father of the movement. Disciples embrace the writings of Pierre Teilhard de Chardin, Henri Bergeson, and William Temple. Some consider John Cobb's **God and the World** to be the best book on the subject.

For many, however, the word *process* means a step-by-step procedure that culminates in a specific result, like a chemical reaction. Scientists and lawyers are among those who may fall into this category. Because the word *process* has different associations among different people, it may be best not to emphasize it when speaking about discernment.

11. This does not mean that *only* those people who have an intimate relationship with God will be called by God or will be able to hear such a call. For example,

Moses' relationship with God seemed to follow from, not precede, his call. Like Moses in his early life, many of us are in the beginning stages of our spiritual relationship with God, not yet close, not yet trusting, not having an intimate relationship—yet wanting to hear God's call. The call to Moses is a reminder that, despite our timidity, we can hear God's voice, even if it seems that a great gulf now separates us from God:

> . . . who [in the Bible] besides Jesus really knew which end was up? **Nobody.** Not Moses. Don't tell me Moses. He was a nice man, and he kept in beautiful touch with his God, and all that—but that's exactly the point. He had to keep in touch. Jesus realized there *is* no separation from God (Salinger, p. 170; emphasis in original).

12. Orsy, p. 182, cautions against using the expression "finding the will of God," noting that "it would take volumes to explicate" its complexities. He explains (pp. 166–67):

> The expression "will of God" carries many meanings, numerous enough to trap the unwary. An attempt to analyze it immediately recalls subtle distinctions between God's positive will and his permissive will. It recalls also the bitter disputes between Dominicans and Jesuits who locked themselves for so long into the wrong question about divine initiative and human freedom. Our purpose here cannot be to undertake a full analysis of past subtleties. But past animosities should make us careful in using the expression. We should remember, too, that many saints did not have or need a scientifically elaborate concept to seek and

to find God's will. Their pilgrimage to [God] did not depend on sophisticated theology.

13. See Orsy (p. 185): "For practical purposes the expression 'seeking and finding the will of God' should be taken as meaning 'to seek and find the next step in the service of the Lord.'"

    Green (p. 96) employs a similar concept in considering the meaning of the Ignatian rules for understanding "to some extent" the movements of the Spirit. The words *to some extent* are Ignatius' words. In Green's view, they are important because God "does not give us a total, long-range blueprint of his will" but rather "reveals his will to us step by step." Tilden Edwards, Episcopal priest, author, and founder of the Shalem Institute in Washington, D.C., suggests that discernment is not discovery of God's will, which "forever remains a mystery," but instead is "aligning ourselves" with God. (Interview, January 30, 1989.)

14. Diocese of Bethlehem, p. 2. Compare Polanyi, p. x: "Things which we can tell, we know by observing them; those that we cannot tell, we know by dwelling in them."

15. Diocese of Bethlehem, p. 2: "Although discernment involves understanding, it is very delicate and is easily clobbered by too much comprehension, or analytical knowledge."

16. Pascal, *Pascal's Pensées,* p. 78.

17. Quaker Hill Conference Center, *Friends Consultation,* address by Jan Wood, p. 12.

18. Green, p. 66. Compare Burtness, p. 71: "... every facet of life exists in the context of fundamental ambiguity."

19. Dunne, p. 39. A century earlier, John Henry Newman used a similar metaphor:

Lead, kindly Light, amid the encircling gloom,
   Lead thou me on;
The night is dark, and I am far from home,
   Lead thou me on;
Keep thou my feet: I do not ask to see
The distant scene; one step enough for me ...

Newman, "Lead, Kindly Light," pp. 74f. Many hymnals contain this poem in the form of a hymn. See, for example, **Hymnal 1940,** Hymn 430.

20. Green, p. 96.
21. Called to resist the evil of Nazi Germany, Bonhoeffer wrote, "God ... demands responsible action in a bold venture of faith and promises forgiveness and consolation to the person who becomes a sinner in that venture." **Letters and Papers,** p. 6.
22. Quaker Hill Conference Center, **Friends Consultation,** address by Jan Wood, p. 10.

CHAPTER 4. WHAT CONDITIONS HELP DISCERN GOD'S CALL?

1. Compare Green, p. 55f, "The Climate of Discernment." Green (pp. 58–61) says three qualities are necessary to discern God's call: desire to do God's will, openness to God, and knowledge of God.
2. Green, p. 55, argues that some conditions are "necessary" before a person can even begin to discern, because discernment requires the same "total commitment to the Lord" as Jesus had in relation to his Father. Yet stating that a person must always meet certain conditions and have a total commitment to the Lord in order to discern God's call seems to limit God's power. With God's grace, even the spiritually diffident may come to hear and recognize the Lord's voice and follow where it leads. With God, "all things

are possible" (Mark 10:27). Consequently, while it is fair to say that having some qualities or predispositions for discernment is *helpful,* to say that they are "necessary" may underestimate God. To disqualify ourselves because we do not have specific qualities could cause us to bury our talents in fear rather than risk response to God who calls us. Compare Matt. 25:25.

3. Orsy, pp. 160–61.

4. Orsy, p. 158. See Toner, p. 126: "It is a presumption that any group of relatively good Christians can at the drop of the hat enter on discernment of God's will and do it with a few prayers and a lot of hot debate... ."

5. This is not to say that trust in the Lord is easily achieved. Kelsey tells the story of a traveler who came to the edge of a chasm which he could not cross. Suddenly, a tightrope appeared and, on it, an acrobat pushing a wheelbarrow with another man inside. When they reached the side where the traveler was standing, the acrobat asked the traveler, "Don't you think I can do it again?" The traveler replied, "Why, yes. I certainly believe you can." The performer asked again. When the answer was the same, he pointed to the wheelbarrow and said, "Good! Then get in and I will take you across." (*The Other Side of Silence*, p. 41.)

For some people, trust comes over time and through experience as they grow in confidence that all things work to the good for those who love God. One aspect of trusting God may be recollecting our past and, in a sense, "forgiving God" for what has gone before. Dunne, p. 58, suggests that a person can suffer all through life from resentment at one's fate and that forgiving God may be "the only way to abolish the hell of this resentment." To make peace with God for the past opens the path of trust in God for the future.

6. See Toner, p. 127.
7. Numerous writers have emphasized the importance of openness in discernment. Ignatius's now-classic description (p. 85) is of an "indifference" to all but God's will:

   ... I must remain indifferent and free from any inordinate attachments so that I am not more inclined or disposed [one way or the other]. I must rather be like the equalized scales of balance, ready to follow the course which ... is more for the glory and praise of God ...

   This concept has come to be known as "Ignatian indifference."
8. de Waal, p. 43.
9. Green, p. 59. See Toner, p. 129: "Consciously admitted ignorance about the right answer to the question at issue is the only valid starting point for discernment."
10. de Waal, pp. 42, 153. The idea of listening with our bodies may be unfamiliar to some, but it is not difficult to understand. For example, if our bodies tell us that we are tired, it may be a sign that we are doing too much. Sanford writes, "Very often ... our body is telling us something because we have not been open to hearing it in any other way" (*Healing and Wholeness,* p. 31).
11. de Waal, p. 43.
12. Authors' (free) translation.
13. de Waal, p. 153.
14. See Teresa of Avila, *Interior Castle,* p. 39.
15. Compare Green, p. 66; Teresa of Avila, *Interior Castle,* pp. 37–39.
16. See *Cloud of Unknowing,* chapters 13 and 14, discussing humility, perfect and imperfect.
17. Compare de Waal, pp. 43, 146; Green, pp. 11–13.

18. Compare Kelsey, *The Other Side of Silence,* pp. 22–23, discussing the various personality types developed by C.J. Jung and their relationship to spiritual development. Among other things, Kelsey suggests that extroverts—persons who find energy and meaning in contact with others—will likely find their prayer life geared to service to others. While this does not mean that extroverts do not need time for quiet and reflection, it may mean that finding such time requires special effort. For a more extended discussion of the relationship between personality type and spiritual life, see Michael and Norrisey.

19. Lewis, *The Screwtape Letters,* p. 49.

20. Bonhoeffer, *Letters and Papers,* p. 169.

21. Quaker Hill Conference Center, *Friends Consultation,* address by Jan Wood, p. 15.

22. Ibid.

23. Ibid.

24. Lewis, *The Screwtape Letters,* p. 132.

25. de Waal, p. 46.

26. Fox, p. 54.

27. Kelsey, *Discernment: A Study in Ecstasy and Evil,* p. 83, distinguishes a person who speaks with authority from a person who thinks he or she has a full grasp of the truth.

28. Compare Dunne, p. 42, discussing the "self-defeating" quality of the pursuit of certainty: the more a person seeks certainty, the more uncertain the person becomes.

Chapter 5. Is It God We Are Hearing?

1. de Waal, p. 105. Compare Teresa of Avila, *Interior Castle,* p. 232:

. . . the devil sometimes puts ambitious desires into our hearts, so that, instead of setting our hand to the work which lies nearest to us, and thus serving Our Lord in ways within our power, we may rest content with having desired the impossible.

2. Compare L'Engle, p. 140:

But neither was Jesus adequate to the situation. He did not feed all the poor, only a few. He did not heal all the lepers, or give sight to all the blind, or drive out all the unclean spirits. Satan wanted him to do all this, but he didn't.

3. de Waal, p. 73.
4. Teilhard de Chardin, **Building the Earth,** p. 76: "... the perfection and usefulness of each nucleus of human energy in relation to the whole depend in the last resort upon whatever is unique and incommunicable in each of them."
5. Quaker Hill Conference Center, **Consultation of Friends,** Howard R. Macy, "Discerning Gifts in Ministry," p. 3: "[G]ifts in ministry may or may not coincide with apparent natural abilities, interests or training."
6. Hammarskjöld, p. 120. Compare Mark 10:27: "With God, all things are possible."
7. God may have many reasons for calling a person to service outside the person's normal skills. For example, a person who is an accountant may constantly be asked to serve on finance committees. Yet God may call the accountant to travel a new road—to act in a play, to take communion to the sick, to work at a shelter—in order to open new doors and bring new growth in the Spirit.

Serving God in an unfamiliar capacity can evoke humility. A talented person who undertakes a task and succeeds may be tempted to take credit for the result; a less-gifted person who undertakes the same task successfully is more likely to see God's hand in it.

8. Compare John of the Cross, p. 606: "If the Spirit of Him who has power descends upon you, do not abandon your place," quoting from Eccles. 10:4.

9. de Waal, p. 62.

10. de Waal, p. 70.

11. John of the Cross, "The Ascent of Mount Carmel" and "Dark Night of the Soul."

12. It is commonly assumed that a spiritual director is the best guide for a person experiencing spiritual darkness. Many spiritual directors, however, are not qualified to provide guidance in this area. For insight into the deficiencies of spiritual directors, see John of the Cross, pp. 626–34. Anyone in the mysterious phase of spiritual darkness will need to seek help patiently, trusting that God will produce a proper guide at the appropriate time.

13. Johnston, p. 116. See also Fenhagen, *Holiness,* p. 45: "The commandments of God have too often been presented in our tradition only as moral precepts by which we can judge our neighbors, rather than as a vision in which the call to holiness is rooted. Our concern is not to have presented to us a blueprint for life that will allow us to avoid risk, but rather a vision of integrity from which decisions are made and life is lived."

14. Compare Brown, *Churches,* pp. 133–34. Brown cites Jesus' willingness to pay the temple tax despite having no obligation to do so as an example of refraining from asserting a principle in order to avoid giving offense (Matt. 17:24–27). He suggests

that a willingness to forgo insistence on a principle is especially important where a threat or challenge to personal prestige may be involved. The same reasoning can be applied to moral principles, especially where, on reflection, pastoral concerns outweigh the principle advanced.

15. God's call transcends moral rules. See, for example, Kierkegaard, *Fear and Trembling,* p. 77, reflecting on the paradox of God's apparently calling Abraham to murder his son, Isaac. Unless Abraham, acting on faith, silenced or disobeyed the moral rule against murder—in what Kierkegaard (p. 77) calls "a teleological suspension of the ethical"—he could not have heard or obeyed God's call to obedience.

    Compare St. Paul's discussion of how faith in God replaces the law:

    > Before this faith came, we were close prisoners in the custody of law, pending the revelation of faith. The law was thus put in charge of us until Christ should come, when we should be justified through faith; and now that faith has come, its charge is at an end. (Gal. 3:23–25, NEB)

    More recently, theologians have discussed the inability of moral rules to address the facts and circumstances of situations in which we need to listen for God's call. See, for example, Burtness, p. 54: "Ethical 'principles' miscarry. They are not after all able to master reality at the decisive moment."

16. Compare Ignatius of Loyola, p. 85. The fourth point in Ignatius' first method of making a wise and good choice is to examine the advantages and disadvantages of a proposed action and, alternatively, the advantages and disadvantages of not taking the action.

17. Futrell, *Ignatian Discernment,* p. 81.
18. Compare Green, p. 31. Green states that God is faithful and cannot contradict God's self. This is helpful to consider in situations where we are receiving seemingly conflicting messages about a call. The danger in using consistency as a guideline for discernment is that we may end up ascribing our human, limited view of consistency to what God is doing. God's purpose for us can be like a shoot emerging from the ground in early spring. The shoot does not resemble the daffodil it will one day become; it is not, in form, texture, or quality, the same as the flower. Yet, in unity of growth, it brings forth the flower. By imposing our own external sense of unity and spiritual growth on God, we may miss a flowering of God's call simply because we view it as inconsistent with the stalk that has come before.

    Nevertheless, God may be telling us something through the apparently conflicting evidence. If we take time to ponder the possibilities, we may be led to new insights.
19. McNeill, Morrisson, and Nouwen, throughout. Compare Fox, p. 121: "The poor are all too often left to God. Therefore, forget those who are better placed and remember the poor."
20. Compare Teresa of Avila, *Life,* p. 239.
21. Compare Brown, *Churches,* p. 44.
22. Ibid., p. 150.
23. Ibid., p. 113. In another book, *Crucified Christ,* Brown gives an example of the need to consider the context of Scriptural writings. In *Crucified Christ,* he notes (pp. 15, 62–63) that the passion narratives of Matthew and John were written at the end of the first century, a time of tremendous hostility between early Christians and Jews. He urges all who preach

during Holy Week to clearly inform congregations
of the context of these passion accounts so that their
implicit message of anti-Semitism does not go unex-
plained. Brown writes (p. 16):

> Sooner or later Christian believers must wrestle
> with the limitations imposed on the Scriptures
> by the circumstances in which they were written.
> They must be brought to see that some attitudes
> found in the Scriptures, however explicable in
> the times in which they originated, may be wrong
> attitudes if repeated today. They must reckon with
> the implications inherent in the fact that God has
> revealed *in words of men.* [Emphasis in original]

24. Brown, **Churches,** pp. 40–41.
25. Ibid., p. 108.
26. Ibid., p. 88 n. 128. Compare John 13:3–5.
27. Compare Fox, p. 61, quoting Meister Eckhart's view
    that loving God for the sake of outward riches or
    inward consolation is no different from loving a cow
    for its milk, cheese, and profit—such love is not for
    God but is for one's own advantage.
28. Green, p. 171, quoting Julian of Norwich. See
    Futrell, p. 63; Teresa of Avila, **Interior Castle,** p. 91.
29. Compare Ignatius of Loyola, p. 133. See Green, pp.
    168–71.
30. Teresa of Avila, **Interior Castle,** p. 168. Compare
    Lewis, **Surprised by Joy,** p. 18: "... joy is never in
    our power."
31. See Teresa of Avila, **Interior Castle,** p. 188.
    Although Teresa is treating the subject of visions,
    a temporary experience of disorientation followed
    by calm and serenity can accompany other spiritual
    experiences. Commotion arises because what had

served as an apparently satisfactory understanding of matters is being pulled out from under us. Peace follows as a new understanding (founded on a sounder comprehension of reality) emerges to replace the old.

32. Teresa of Avila, *Interior Castle,* p. 167.
33. Futrell, *Ignatian Discernment,* p. 57. "Felt-knowledge" translates the Ignatian concept, *sentir,* which describes the interaction of feelings and thoughts that confirm or question a call. Futrell, p. 56, writes, "It is through attention to one's *sentir,* the vital testimony of profound human feelings during the discernment process, that one discovers the *orientation* of his impulses towards decision or action," and, at the same time, "the *origin* of these impulses" (emphasis in original).
34. Teresa of Avila, *Interior Castle,* p. 185.
35. Compare the Ignatian concept of "consolation without previous cause," which refers to an unsought and unexpected spiritual experience. The experience is so clear that, at the time, there is no doubt of God's presence. See Ignatius of Loyola, pp. 133–34; see also Teresa of Avila, *Interior Castle,* p. 141.
36. See Teresa of Avila, *Interior Castle,* pp. 150–51, 179–80, 185. See also Teresa of Avila, *Life,* p. 236: "...the Lord impresses His words upon the memory so that it is impossible to forget them...."
37. de Waal, p. 137.
38. Compare Ignatius of Loyola, p. 130.
39. In an August 30, 1990, letter, David A. Scott, ethics professor at the Virginia Theological Seminary, expressed his admiration for students who deferred seminary study because of family commitments. Scott is concerned about accepting single parents as

students who would spend "even less time than they might with their small children."

40. Conversation, June 5, 1989, with Michael J. Sheeran, S.J., vice president of academic affairs of Regis College in Denver, Colorado, and author of *Beyond Majority Rule.*

41. Fox, p. 32: "People who dwell in God dwell in the eternal now"; Lewis, *Mere Christianity,* pp. 146–47. See generally Tillich, *The Eternal Now,* pp. 122–32.

42. Johnston, p. 117.

43. Kelsey, *Discernment: A Study in Ecstasy and Evil,* p. 83.

44. See Green, chapters 6 and 7.

CHAPTER 6. WHY IS CHRISTIAN COMMUNITY IMPORTANT IN DISCERNING GOD'S CALL?

1. Compare John of the Cross, p. 132: God "draws near to those who come together in an endeavor to know" the truth.

2. Bonhoeffer, *Letters and Papers,* pp. 236–37: "I feel that it's one of the laws of spiritual understanding that one's own thoughts, when they are understood by others, at the same time always undergo a transformation and liberation through the medium of the person."

3. John of the Cross, p. 184.

4. See John of the Cross, p. 184. John of the Cross discusses this in relation to a spiritual director, but others trained in the area of discernment can also help a person seeking discernment. Compare Futrell, *Ignatian Discernment,* p. 55, discussing Ignatius' emphasis on the need to consult with others in proportion to the complexity of the issue.

5. John of the Cross, p. 182, states that God does not want us to bestow entire credence on his communications, or be confirmed in their strength and security, until they pass through the human channel of the mouth of another person.
6. Woolman, throughout.
7. Ibid.
8. Compare Teilhard de Chardin, **Building the Earth,** p. 81, discussing the powers of the universe that "gradually assume the form of a fundamental affinity which links individuals to each other and to their transcendent Center."

CHAPTER 7. THE VALUE OF A DISCERNMENT GROUP

1. Compare Futrell, **Communal Discernment,** p. 177. Paraphrasing Carl Rogers, Futrell writes that one reason people find it so hard to really listen to one another is that when they do, there is always a possibility of having to change—which all of us tend to fear and resist.
2. Tillich, **Love, Power, and Justice,** p. 84.
3. See Futrell, **Communal Discernment,** p. 173: "The entire process of spiritual discernment is prayer. Consequently, it is vital to establish an atmosphere of prayer, of openness to the Holy Spirit and to one another." See also Futrell, **Ignatian Discernment,** p. 72: "Failure in communal discernment most often is the result of the fact that the [persons] engaging in the discernment do not pray. It is as simple—and as difficult—as that."
4. Bonhoeffer, **Life Together,** p. 79.
5. Bonhoeffer, **Life Together,** p. 80. While Scripture, intuition, and experience have taught Christians the value of silence, recent experiments in education

document the salutary effects of increased silence, or "wait time," in a classroom. See Rowe; Swift and Gooding; and Tobin. Wait time refers to (1) deliberately increased amounts of time a teacher allows between asking a question and expecting a response, and (2) deliberately extended lengths of time a teacher permits a student to pause when responding to a question before determining that the student has finished. These experiments show that as the pace of interchange in a classroom slows down, the quality of the teacher's questions increases; the quality of the students' participation goes up; the level of thinking in the class rises; the number of students taking part in class discussion increases; the way students listen to each other improves; and discipline problems decrease.

6. **Consensus** means the sense of the group. **Sense of the meeting** is a Quaker term that has a spiritual connotation suggesting a settled place to which the Holy Spirit has led the group; it is sought through silence and listening together, unhampered by preconceived opinions. **Unity** and **concord** are other terms that Quakers sometimes use interchangeably with **sense of the meeting.**

7. For a fuller discussion of spiritual consensus, see Farnham, Hull, and McLean, chapter 6.

Chapter 8. Supporting the Ministries of Others

1. In a letter of November 5, 1990, James Fenhagen, dean of the General Theological Seminary, went so far as to say, "Never call someone for ministry until a system of support has been established."

Epilogue

1. Rilke, pp. 34–35.

Appendix 1. Guidelines for Discernment Groups

1. The starting point for these guidelines was a set of procedures for a Quaker clearness committee drawn up by the noted Quaker, Parker Palmer. These procedures were used and distributed at a conference entitled "Solitude and Community" at Kirkridge Retreat and Study Center in Bangor, PA, April 1987.
2. The term *focus person* comes from the Quakers. It carries the advantage of having no other connotations.

Appendix 2. Types of Questions to Raise When Serving in Discernment Groups

1. Merton, *The Seven Storey Mountain,* pp. 139–40.

Annotated Bibliography

Unless otherwise noted, Scripture quotations are from the New Revised Standard Version Bible. Other versions are indicated throughout book by the following abbreviations:

JB: Jerusalem Bible
KJV: King James Version
NIV: New International Version
REB: Revised English Bible
TNIV: Today's New International Version

Author Unknown, *The Cloud of Unknowing* and *The Book of Privy*

Written by an anonymous English mystic of the fourteenth century, these two works address the person who feels drawn to contemplative prayer. They contain invaluable guidance for anyone trying to discern a call to contemplation.

Bacon, Margaret Hope. *Mothers of Feminism: The Story of Quaker Women in America.* New York: Harper & Row, 1986.

This book shows how a handful of dedicated people living out their sense of call exerted influence far greater than their numbers. These Quaker women serve as an inspiration, reminding us that we can have an important impact when we act from our Christian conviction. Historical and fascinating.

Bacovin, Helen, trans. *The Way of a Pilgrim.* Garden City, NY: Doubleday, 1978.

The story of a Russian peasant who, upon hearing the exhortation in Paul's First Letter to the Thessalonians to "pray constantly," is filled with a deep desire to know what this means. Of this desire he is told, "Recognize in this a call from God and be at peace." He learns the Jesus prayer, "Lord Jesus Christ, have mercy on me," and travels his entire life from place to place, saying the prayer with lips and heart, sharing the prayer with others.

Barclay, William. A translation of *The Gospel of Matthew* with an introduction and interpretation, vol. 2 (chaps. 11 to 28). Revised edition. *The Daily Study Bible Series.* Philadelphia: Westminister Press, 1975.

Benedict. *The Rule of St. Benedict.* Translated by Anthony C. Meisel and M. L. del Mastro. Garden City, NY: Doubleday, 1975.

Discusses persuasively the importance of meeting in community to consider significant matters and of providing support for one another's work. Also points out the value of hearing from the least seasoned members of the community as well as the contribution of a balanced and well-ordered life.

Bonhoeffer, Dietrich.

Bonhoeffer's theology, written in the cauldron that was Nazi Germany of the 1930s and 1940s, has continued to inspire, shape, and direct Christian concern and action for social and international justice ever since.

Letters and Papers from Prison. Edited by Eberhard Bethge. New York: Macmillan, 1979.

Confronts us with God's call to assume a share of responsibility for the course of history.

Life Together. Translated by John W. Doberstein. New York: Harper & Row, 1954.

Defines Christianity as community through and in Jesus Christ. Useful discussions are found on the importance and use of silence, the value and content of meditation, and the ministry of listening.

The Cost of Discipleship. Revised edition. Translated by R. H. Fuller, with some revision by Irmgard Booth. New York: Macmillan, 1963.

Focuses on Jesus and his call to us to be disciples. "What is his will for us today?" Bonhoeffer asks, "What [is it] Jesus Christ himself wants us to do?" And, he asks, "if we answer the call to discipleship, where will it lead us? What decisions and partings will it demand?" This book is important for anyone seeking to respond to God's call.

The Book of Common Prayer. New York: Church Publishing, 1979.

Broholm, Richard R. **Toward Claiming and Identifying Our Ministry in the Workplace.** Newton Center, MA: Center for the Ministry of the Laity, Andover Newton Theological School, n.d.

Brown, Raymond E. *The Churches the Apostles Left Behind.* New York: Paulist, 1984.

Brown's scholarly grasp of Scripture and of life in the apostolic era is unparalleled. This book is an important resource on Scripture and Christian community.

A Crucified Christ in Holy Week: Essays on the Four Gospel Passion Narratives. Collegeville, MN: Liturgical Press, 1986.

Meditations on the differing accounts of Jesus' suffering and death. Helpful discussion of the context in which Scripture was written. Excellent Lenten reading.

Brown, Raymond E., and John P. Meier. *Antioch and Rome: New Testament Cradles of Catholic Christianity.* New York: Paulist, 1983.

This exploration of diversity and dissension in the early church provides guidance for those trying to discern God's call in circumstances of conflict.

Buber, Martin. *The Writings of Martin Buber.* Cleveland: World, 1969.

Burtness, James H. *Shaping the Future: The Ethics of Dietrich Bonhoeffer.* Philadelphia: Fortress, 1985.

A wealth of important material. The thesis: life is always filled with ambiguity, but we need to assume responsibility. We need to take action after earnestly looking at our situation at a given time and place, considering the consequences of action or lack of it, examining our hearts, and giving due weight to the reality of God and the world together in Christ.

The Cloud of Unknowing and *The Book of Privy Counseling.* Edited by William Johnston. Garden City, NY: Doubleday, 1973.

Written by an anonymous English mystic of the fourteenth century, these two works address the person who feels drawn to contemplative prayer. They contain invaluable guidance for anyone trying to discern a call to contemplation.

Cobb, John. *God and the World.* Philadelphia: Westminister Press, 1969.

de Waal, Esther. *Seeking God: The Way of St. Benedict.* Collegeville, MN: Liturgical Press, 1984.

Esther de Waal is an English historian whose extraordinary insight into the Rule of St. Benedict brings Benedictine principles of spirituality alive to ordinary people for their daily life. This book is filled with wisdom that is valuable in discernment.

Diehl, William E. *Christianity and Real Life.* Philadelphia: Fortress, 1976.

A discussion of moral dilemmas and how the church speaks to them. Makes a case for the ministry of the laity.

Diocese of Bethlehem (Pennsylvania) of the Episcopal Church. *The Manual of Policies, Guidelines, and Requirements for Seeking the Ordained Ministry.* Accompanied by "Additional Guidelines for the Parish Discernment Fellowship." Bethlehem, PA: Diocese of Bethlehem, 1984.

Dunne, John S. *The Way of All the Earth: Experiments in Truth and Religion.* Notre Dame, IN: University of Notre Dame Press, 1972.

An original thinker gathers insights offered by other religions and applies them to the Christian journey with God. Rich in descriptions to help us see our lives as spiritual adventures with God as our companion.

Eliot, T.S. *Four Quartets.* New York: Harcourt Brace Jovanovich, 1971.

A small book of poems exploring remembered experience in life's pilgrimage toward God.

Farnham, Suzanne G., Stephanie A. Hull, and R. Taylor McLean. *Grounded in God: Listening Hearts Discernment for Group Deliberations.* Harrisburg, PA: Morehouse Publishing, 1996.

Explains spiritual discernment as it relates to seeking God's guidance for group decision-making. Appendices provide step-by-step suggestions for implementing the ideas presented.

Fenhagen, James C. *Invitation to Holiness.* Harrisburg, PA: Morehouse Publishing, 1991.

Here we find the disturbing thought that Christians are called not to virtue but to service in and for the world in companionship with each other and the Lord. A section on spiritual direction is helpful for those not familiar with the term. Sections on vocation, the importance of framing and considering questions without insisting on immediate answers, and the purpose of the worshiping community are also of special relevance to those committed to discerning God's call in community.

Mutual Ministry: New Vitality for the Local Church. New York: Seabury, 1977.

This down-to-earth book helps prepare a foundation for mutual ministry in the parish.

Fox, Matthew. *Meditations with Meister Eckhart.* Santa Fe, NM: Bear & Company, 1983.

Futrell, John Carroll. *Ignatian Discernment.* Vol. 2, no. 2 of *Studies in the Spirituality of Jesuits.* St. Louis, MO: American Assistancy Seminar on Jesuit Spirituality, 1969.

A primer for understanding the language and meaning of the "Rules for the Discernment of Spirits" section of *The Spiritual Exercises of Ignatius.* The paper strives to teach how to apply Ignatian concepts of discernment to situations of everyday life.

Futrell. *Communal Discernment: Reflections on Experience.* Vol. 4, no. 5 of *Studies in the Spirituality of Jesuits.* St. Louis, MO: American Assistancy Seminar on Jesuit Spirituality, 1972.

Applies Ignatian concepts of discernment to communities seeking discernment of God's call to the community.

Green, Thomas H. *Weeds among the Wheat: Where Prayer and Action Meet.* Notre Dame, IN: Ave Maria Press, 1984.

This work by a Jesuit provides an excellent synthesis of Ignatian discernment with a good bit of Carmelite spirituality sprinkled in.

Hammerskjöld, Dag. *Markings.* Translated by Leif Sjoberg and W. H. Auden. New York: Knopf, 1964.

This spiritual diary of the former secretary general of the United Nations is a good resource for reflective prayer.

Heron, Alastair. *Gifts and Ministries: A Discussion Paper on Eldership.* London: Quaker Home Service, 1987.

This paper about an issue close to the Quaker community offers valuable insight into questions of mutual responsibility that arise in any Christian community.

Holl, Karl. "The History of the Word Vocation *(Beruf).*" Translated by Herber F. Peacock. Baltimore, MD: Listening Hearts Ministries, unpublished paper.

The Hymnal of the Protestant Episcopal Church in the United States of America: 1940. New York: Church Pension Fund, 1940.

Ignatius of Loyola. *The Spiritual Exercises of St. Ignatius.* Translated by Anthony Mottola. Garden City, NY: Doubleday, 1964.

This classic, highly intellectual work of spirituality contains Ignatius' chief work on discernment, "Rules for the Discernment of Spirits." Related chapters include "Introduction to Making a Choice of a Way of Life."

John of the Cross. *The Collected Works of John the Cross.* Translated by Kieran Kavanaugh, O.C.D., and Otilio Rodriguez, O.C.D. Washington, DC: Institute of Carmelite Studies Publications, 1976.

The author, a sixteenth-century mystic and cofounder of the Discalced Carmelites, speaks to the Christian who has a disciplined prayer life and a bent for contemplative prayer. Those with inadequate background risk the danger of misconstruing what he says. The first two books in this volume, *The Ascent of Mount Carmel* and *The Dark Night,* are gold mines of insight on discernment. They combine to form one work expounding upon his poem, "The Dark Night," one of the finest poems of Spanish literature.

The Living Flame of Love, another book in the collection, speaks especially to one seeking discernment in a period of intense spiritual transformation.

Johnston, William. *The Still Point: Reflections on Zen and Christian Mysticism.* New York: Fordham University Press, 1970.

The Zen perspective explored in this work can help the Christian prepare to approach discernment with heart and mind unencumbered.

Julian of Norwich. *Revelations of Divine Love.* Translated into modern English by Clifton Wolters. Harmondsworth, England: Penguin, 1966.

These meditations on visions of God show an entire life enfolded in God's love.

Jung, Carl G. "Psychotherapists or the Clergy." In *Psychology and Religion: West and East.* Translated by R. F. C. Hull. Princeton, NJ: Princeton University Press, 1969.

Kelsey, Morton. *Discernment: A Study in Ecstasy and Evil.* New York: Paulist, 1978.

The Other Side of Silence. Paramus, NJ: Paulist Press, 1976.

A practical guide to Christian meditation that includes discussion on practicing silence and using images.

Kierkegaard, Søren. *A Kierkegaard Anthology.* Edited by Robert Bretail. Princeton, NJ: Princeton University Press, 1946.

Fear and Trembling with *Sickness Unto Death.*
Princeton, NJ: Princeton University Press, 1954.

Lawrence, Brother [Nicolas Herman, 1611–91]. *The Practice of the Presence of God.* Cincinnati: Forward Movement Publications.

The spirit of a Carmelite kitchen brother of the seventeenth century who lived his life as prayer, emanates from the pages of this short book. Ultimately, discernment depends on a close personal relationship with God; this book helps to lay the groundwork for that to develop.

L'Engle, Madeleine. *The Irrational Season.* San Francisco: Harper & Row, 1977.

Lewis, C.S. *The Great Divorce.* New York: Macmillan, 1946.

Herein lie some pithy insights of value in discernment.

Mere Christianity. New York: Collier Books, Macmillan, 1952.

The author's classic defense of Christianity. In a short section "Beyond Personality," Lewis provides perspective on the human concept of time, which has relevance for discernment.

The Screwtape Letters: How a Senior Devil Instructs a Junior Devil in the Art of Temptation. New York: Macmillan, 1961.

Lewis's great ironic work on how good and evil operate in the world and on how to distinguish between them.

Surprised by Joy. New York: Harcourt Brace Jovanovich, 1955.

Luther, Martin. *Martin Luther: Selections from His
Writings.* Edited by John Dillenberger. Garden
City, NY: Anchor, 1961.

May, Gerald G. *Addiction and Grace.* San Francisco:
Harper & Row, 1988.

A new way of looking at what classical spirituality
calls "detachment."

McNeill, Donald P., Douglas A. Morrison, and Henri
J. M. Nouwen. *Compassion: A Reflection on the
Christian Life.* Garden City, NY: Doubleday, 1982.

Helpful discussions on obedience, on the distinction between vocation and career, and on community as it relates to ministry make this a good book
on servanthood.

Merton, Thomas. *New Seeds of Contemplation.* New
York: New Directions, 1972.

One of Merton's most widely read works, this book
offers profound reflections on humility, obedience,
detachment, personal identity, and contemplative
experience.

The Seven Storey Mountain. New York: Harcourt
Brace Jovanovich, 1948.

Thoughts in Solitude. New York: Farrar, Straus and
Giroux, 1958.

Michael, Chester P., and Marie C. Norrisey. *Prayer and
Temperament: Different Prayer Forms for Different*

Personality Types. Charlottesville, VA. Open Door, 1984.

Explaining the varied spiritual needs of different people, this book explores why what works for one person may not work for the next. Understanding these differences is helpful for discerners.

Newman, John Henry. *A Newman Reader.* Edited by Francis X. Connelly. Garden City, NY: Doubleday, 1964.

O'Conner, Elizabeth. *Journey Inward, Journey Outward.* San Francisco: Harper & Row, 1968.

Orsy, Ladislas. *Toward a Theological Evaluation of Communal Discernment.* Vol. 5, no. 5 of *Studies in the Spirituality of Jesuits.* St. Louis, MO: American Assistancy Seminar on Jesuit Spirituality, 1972.

Palmer, Parker J. *A Place Called Community.* Pendle Hill Pamphlet 212. Wallingford, PA: Pendle Hill, 1977.

Recommended reading on community.

A Hidden Wholeness: The Journey Toward an Undivided Life. San Francisco, John Wiley & Sons, 2004.

Filled with profound insights and practical wisdom applicable to Listening Hearts discernment groups, this work is a solid resource for anyone interested in spiritual discernment.

Let Your Life Speak: Listening for the Voice of Vocation. San Francisco, John Wiley & Sons, 2000.

This book is laced with reflections relevant to finding one's true self.

The Promise of Paradox: A Celebration of Contradictions in the Christian Life. Introduction by Henri Nouwen. San Francisco, John Wiley & Sons, 2008.

The first three chapters of this work shed light on the value of holding apparently opposite truths in creative tension until a larger truth emerges.

Pascal, Blaise. *Pascal's Pensees,* trans. by W. F. Trotter. New York: E.P. Dutton & Co., 1958.

Peck, George, and John S. Hoffman, eds. *The Laity in Ministry.* Valley Forge, PA: Judson Press, 1984.

Challenges Christians to envision ministry with new eyes, using a fresh vocabulary.

Polanyi, Michael. *Personal Knowledge.* New York: Harper & Row, 1964.

Pronzato, Allessandro. *Meditations on the Sand.* Translated by Thomas Kala. New York: Alba House, 1983.

A reflective look at our concept of time and the way we relate to our culture and material possessions.

Quaker Hill Conference Center. *Consultation of Friends on Ministry: Discerning, Nurturing, Recording and Releasing.* Richmond, IN: Quaker Hill Conference Center, 1981.

Friends Consultation on Discernment. Richmond, IN: Quaker Hill Conference Center, 1985.

Papers by Quaker writers on discernment. Of these, Jan Woods "Spiritual Discernment: The Personal Dimension" is singularly inspiring, a work of poetic prose describing some of the characteristics of a life discerned in God.

Friends Consultation on Spiritual Authority and Accountability. Richmond, IN: Quaker Hill Conference Center, 1984.

An excellent resource on the relationship between authority and accountability.

Rilke, Rainer Maria. **Letters to a Young Poet.** Translated by Stephen Mitchell. New York: Random House, 1984.

Rohr, Richard. **The Naked Now**. New York: The Crossroad Publishing Company, 2009.

Although discernment is not an explicit topic, this book leaves no doubt that it is the Lord's direction, not his acquiescence, we are seeking. For instance, Rohr's words on spirituality apply with equal force to discernment: "The core task of all good spirituality [discernment] is to teach us to 'cooperate' with what God already wants to do.... We are always and forever merely seconding the motion" (p. 23). The same applies to his words on prayer: "... true prayer [discernment] stops defending or promoting its ideas and feelings, lets go of any antagonistic attitudes or fears, and waits for, expects, and receives guidance from Another" (p. 102). There are also many other expressions throughout the book that provide insight and guidance for those who are seeking to be listening hearts, grounded in God.

Rowe, Mary Budd. *Teaching Science as Continuous Inquiry.* New York: McGraw-Hill, 1973.

Salinger, J.D. *Franny and Zooey.* New York: Bantam Books, 1964.

Sanford, John. *Dreams: God's Forgotten Language.* San Francisco: Harper & Row, 1989.

An Episcopal priest who is a Jungian analyst writes about the use of dreams in the Christian spiritual life. Although discerners do not necessarily use dreams in conjunction with their prayer life, it is important that they be able to listen receptively to those who do.

Healing and Wholeness. New York: Paulist, 1977.

Explores the relationship between our health and our life in God.

Sedgwick, Timothy F. "Making the Connections: Developing the Ministry of the Laity." *Ministry Development Journal* (no. 17, 1989): 3–7.

Servant Leadership School Program Offerings, Fall 1990. Washington, DC.

The Servant Leadership School is an ecumenical center for theological reflection and spiritual formation located in Washington, DC. The school seeks to address what it calls "the most pressing need of our time – the need for compassionate, spiritually grounded leadership." For more information, go to www.slchool.org.

Sheeran, Michael J. *Beyond Majority Rule: Voteless Decisions in the Religious Society of Friends.* Philadelphia: Philadelphia Yearly Meeting, 1983.

This book about the Quakers is written by a Jesuit. It is a primary book Quakers suggest for those interested in the Quaker decision-making process. Since procedures for discernment put forth in *Listening Hearts* are based on a Quaker model, this book is important background reading for discerners.

Swift, Nathan J., and C. Thomas Gooding. "Interaction of Wait Time Feedback and Questioning Instruction on Middle School Science Teaching." *Journal of Research in Science Teaching,* 20 (no. 8, 1983): 721–30.

Teilhard de Chardin, Pierre. *Building the Earth.* Denville, NJ: Dimension Books, 1965.

Compared to his other works, this book is easy to read and contains many of the ideas found in Teilhard's more ponderous *The Phenomenon of Man.* His comprehension of the unity of all creation and the interconnectedness of all things is helpful to discerning God's voice.

Teresa of Avila. *Interior Castle.* Translated and edited by E. Allison Peers. Garden City, NY: Doubleday, 1961.

In this work, Teresa combines an unpretentious style with profound insight into call and discernment.

The Life of Teresa of Jesus: The Autobiography of St. Teresa of Avila. Translated and edited by E. Allison Peers. Garden City, NY: Doubleday, 1960.

Long and difficult reading, but filled with wisdom of value to the discerner.

Tillich, Paul. *The Eternal Now.* New York: Charles Scribner's Sons, 1963.

Of particular import to the discerner is Tillich's exposition on time found in the title chapter, "The Eternal Now."

Love, Power, and Justice. New York: Oxford University Press, 1954.

Evocative. Concise. Meaty. Understanding the relationships among love, power, and justice can be of great importance in discerning God's call.

Tobin, Kenneth. "Effects of Extended Wait Time on Discourse Characteristics and Achievements in Middle School Grades." *Journal of Research in Science Teaching,* 21 (no. 8, 1984): 779–91.

Toner, Jules J. *A Method for Communal Discernment of God's Will.* Vol. 3, no. 4 of *Studies in the Spirituality of Jesuits.* St. Louis, MO: American Assistancy Seminar on Jesuit Spirituality, 1971.

Ulanov, Ann, and Barry Ulanov. *Primary Speech.* Atlanta: John Knox Press, 1982.

Vanauken, Sheldon. *A Severe Mercy.* San Francisco: Harper & Row, 1977.

Personal letters of advice from C.S. Lewis highlight this autobiographical work, which casts light on the relationship between personal loss and spiritual growth.

Vanier, Jean. *Community and Growth.* New York: Paulist, 1979.

Readable and practical, this book reflects true-life experience in responding to call.

Vos, Nelvin. *Monday's Ministries: The Ministry of the Laity.* Philadelphia: Parish Life, 1979.

Suitable for an adult or senior high class, this book emphasizes that ministry is personal and found in everyday life.

Ware, Timothy, ed. *The Art of Prayer: An Orthodox Anthology.* London: Faber & Faber, 1966.

This collection of excerpts on the prayer of the heart is from the Orthodox tradition.

Weil, Simone. *Waiting for God.* New York: Harper & Row, 1951.

Whitehead, James D., and Evelyn Eaton Whitehead. *The Emerging Laity: Returning Leadership to the Community of Faith.* Garden City, NY: Doubleday, 1986.

As a team, the Whiteheads bring a background in theology, psychology, and church history. They make a strong case for shared leadership in the church.

Williams, H.A. *Some Day I'll Find You.* London: Mitchell Beazley Condon, 1982.

Woolman, John. *The Journals and Major Essays of John Woolman.* Edited by Phillips P. Moulton.

Richmond, IN: Friends United Press, 1989. Reprint of Oxford University Press edition, 1971.

If the Quakers have provided a model for discerning God's call in community, John Woolman serves as its personification. One could find no better book than this to tell what discernment in community has meant in the life of a particular person.

Wright, N.T. *The Challenge of Jesus*. Downers Grove, IL, 1999.

Bishop Wright identifies love as a basic mode of knowing, "with the love of God as the highest and fullest sort of knowing that there is." In place of what Wright refers to as "the hermeneutics of suspicion" that he says characterize the current age, "[w]e need to articulate, for the post-postmodern world, what we might call an epistemology of love." He makes this point with language from the hymn, "Once In Royal David's City": "And our eyes at last shall see him, through his own redeeming love" and closes with his own poem (p. 197):

Let me trust, and see,
And let love's eyes pursue
and set me free.

Glossary

Discernment Terminology

A Glossary by Category

Different strands of spirituality and different people employ different terminology when discussing discernment. In some cases, two or more terms may have essentially the same meaning. In other cases, words may have similar meanings, but with definite distinctions. The list that follows has been assembled to help people navigate readings and discussions that relate to discernment. It is arranged by category so the reader can easily compare terms that are similar or closely related.

Calling

The Spirit of love and truth is continually drawing us to behave in a way that is authentic to the person we are created to be. This applies to the overall direction of our lives as well as to the choices we make as we live life from day to day. In his book *Let Your Life Speak*, Parker Palmer offers an insightful exploration of this subject based on his own personal pilgrimage.

Call

God continually tries to guide us and communicate with us through the events, situations, and relationships of our life—through our thoughts, feelings, senses, imagination, and intuition. This can be understood as God's voice or God's call.

The heart

The heart in Hebrew-Christian tradition has more than a physical nature. It is seen as the core of the person, in the center of the body, encompassing the mind, soul, and spirit.

Ministry

When we respond to God's call, what we do as a positive response is considered ministry. This includes the way we relate to people at home, in the workplace, in the church, and in the wider community, as well as ways in which we reach out to address the needs of all creation. For some persons, this includes a professional vocation in the church.

The self

Carl Jung referred to the true center of one's being as the self. This is the place within which all aspects of one's being, dark and light, are integrated and in harmony. As a person moves toward the self, one is pursuing God's call.

True self

As one lives in an intimate relationship with God, following where God leads, a person becomes more and more fully one's true self, in effect living in accordance with one's call.

Vocation

Vocation comes from the Latin word that means call and usually refers to the overall focus meant for one's life. Often it is used to refer to the work of an ordained person, but it is by no means limited to those considered "professional" ministers.

Discernment

The verb "to discern" – meaning to sort out, to sift through, to distinguish – is widely used in the secular world as well as in the church. The noun "discernment," however, is used almost exclusively in religious circles, but suggests different things to different groups of people. In order to avoid confusion, it is helpful to specify the type of discernment one is talking about.

Discernment of call

This is an effort to distinguish the voice of God from other voices that tell us what to do, such as the voice of our parents echoing through the years, voices of teachers and mentors who have been important to us, voices of friends, civic leaders, and religious leaders; voices from nature, art, music, literature, and the media. Often God does speak to us through these voices, but not everything they say is God's word for us. And what is God's call in one time and place may not be God's call for us in a similar situation in a different context. Discernment of call involves sorting out the voices.

Discernment of gifts

It is important to know what our gifts are so that we can make conscious use of them and be appropriately thankful. Gift discernment is scriptural. But God often calls us to do things that we do not appear to be qualified to accomplish. In fact, God is inclined to call people to do things for which they seem ill suited. Consider Sarah and Abraham, the childless couple in their old age, being called to become progenitors of an entire race of people. Or Moses, a man with a speech impediment wanted on charges of murder in Egypt, being chosen to go to Pharaoh to plead on behalf of the Hebrews. Throughout the Bible we see examples of people setting out to do what seems impossible, doing so because God has commanded them and they obey. It is only after they step forward in trusting obedience that God gives them what they need to accomplish the task.

Discernment of spirits (*diakrisis pneumaton*)

This is the term that St. Ignatius of Loyola used to connote distinguishing the Spirit of God from other spirits that influence us: the spirit of the times, the spirit of a nation, the spirit of excelling, of winning, of succeeding. Discernment of spirits and discernment of call are essentially the same thing, using a different vocabulary.

Rational discernment in a Christian context

This is the kind of discernment that most Christians use. Typically, it begins and ends with prayers, proceeds with study, discussion, and/or debate, applying Christian principles to arrive at what is essentially a rational decision.

Spiritual discernment

This begins with rational discernment in a Christian context, but goes beyond that to offer ourselves and any preliminary conclusion to God to be taken wherever the Spirit may lead. It involves becoming still, open to God, and not clinging to anything (personal relationships, material possessions, thoughts, feelings, opinions, convictions, or concepts of God) in order to become supple in God's hands and open to the action of the Holy Spirit. It is essentially contemplative prayer, surrendering all to the flow of the Holy Spirit.

PEOPLE APPOINTED TO HELP A PERSON WHO SEEKS GOD'S GUIDANCE

Different terms are used by different groups to designate people who assist others in looking for divine guidance. Some traditions use professionals, others use trained non-professionals. Still others require no specific training.

Clearness committee

In most Friends meetings, any member who is wrestling with a concern or issue may request a group to gather with them Quaker style (sitting in stillness, alert to the inner light that burns within each person, speaking only when urged by the Spirit of God, patiently waiting for the light within those present to merge and bring unity) to help develop clarity in handling it. Usually the group consists of between four and six members of the meeting.

Director

Ignatian discernment is guided by a director who is schooled in discernment of spirits based on the teachings of St. Ignatius of Loyola, who founded the Society of Jesus, commonly known as Jesuits.

Discerner

Members of a Listening Hearts discernment group are referred to as discerners.

Discernment group

Some discernment groups are formed to help a particular person with discernment on a continuing and regular basis; such a group is a discernment support group for a particular person. Other groups are formed to meet on a continuing basis to help one another with discernment during regularly scheduled meetings; these are communal discernment support groups. For Listening Hearts discernment, each group is recruited to help a specific person only with a specific issue. The guidelines for a Listening Hearts discernment group are modeled using Parker Palmer's guidelines for a clearness committee. Because the Listening Hearts guidelines do not presuppose familiarity with the culture of the Religious Society of Friends, they are more extensive and recommend trained discerners. They also incorporate wisdom and experience from other spiritual traditions, especially Ignatian and Carmelite.

Spiritual director

A seasoned person of prayer who accompanies an individual as a guide on his or her spiritual journey.

The two usually meet once a month for about an hour, although different arrangements are not uncommon. Many have been trained in formal training programs. Some charge fees; others do not.

A PERSON SEEKING DISCERNMENT

Anyone who yearns to do what God would have him or her do, either in a specific situation or in a more comprehensive sense, is seeking discernment. Those who look for structured help in this quest are sometimes referred to with specific terms.

Focus person

A person who requests a Quaker clearness committee. Listening Hearts has adopted the term to apply to a person who asks for a discernment group.

Seeker

In some Listening Hearts programs, the term seeker is used rather than focus person.

LETTING GO

Every contemplative spiritual tradition emphasizes the importance of letting go. Clinging to any thought, feeling, person, or thing is an impediment to being fully open to the divine presence.

Detachment

In spiritual theology, this is the term most commonly used for letting go. It implies not being attached to anything, including our concept of God.

Ignatian indifference

This is a term that Jesuits use for detachment.

Signs of God's Spirit

In spiritual discernment, we look for signs of the Spirit to help us sense the strength of God's presence as we seek to align ourselves with God. Should we misinterpret what God is saying to us, we trust that the Holy Spirit will correct our understanding as long as we continue to travel in close communion with God, drawing us back if we get off the right path. Below are some terms that refer to signs that can help us detect God's participation and are specific to a given tradition.

Consolation without previous cause

This is an Ignatian phrase that connotes a spiritual experience that comes to us unsought and unanticipated. It is an experience of the divine presence so vivid that it leaves no doubt that it was God.

Convergence

When a number of things that had no apparent relationship and occurred over an extended period of time suddenly converge and fit together like a puzzle, this is called convergence.

Felt knowledge (*sentir*)

This Ignatian term refers to a dawning of God's call that can come as one pays close attention to thoughts and feelings from one's depths as they interact to reveal the source of one's impulses toward a decision or action.

Leading

A term used by Quakers when referring to a strong spiritual pull to take a particular action.

Persistence

This connotes that the same message keeps coming to a person at different times through unrelated channels. For instance, the message might first come in the course of a conversation with a friend. A few days later, maybe you are watching TV and get the same message. A month later, you hear a song on the radio that carries the message once again. This can be a sign that God is trying to tell you something.

CONSENSUS

Secular consensus suggests sensing together through rational consideration. No votes are taken, but a resolution is arrived at that everyone can accept, which does not imply unanimity. Spiritual discernment awaits a consensus that includes spiritual harmony.

Concord

This word is found in classic Quaker writings and suggests that spiritual oneness has drawn the group together in relation to the matter under consideration.

Sense of the meeting

In a Quaker meeting for business, a sense of the meeting indicates that there is a shared sense that a particular emerging decision is in accordance with God's will. This is articulated by the clerk for approval by the meeting.

Spiritual consensus

This is a consensus that comes when those present have become knit together through the action of the Holy Spirit and everyone present is at peace with the place at which the group has arrived.

Unity

Gathered in silence, Quakers consider a concern before them by practicing reverent speaking and attentive listening until they arrive at an understanding about the matter under consideration in a manner that brings forth spiritual oneness, which they call unity. This is what some call spiritual consensus.

OTHER RESOURCES FOR PEOPLE SEEKING INSIGHT AND GUIDANCE

There are other places to go for help that dovetail with spiritual discernment. They can provide an alternative to spiritual discernment or be used in conjunction with it.

Pastoral counseling

Pastoral counselors help Christians in search of guidance with problems, not avoiding direct questions, often offering observations and insights.

Psychological counseling

Psychological counselors help people explore their inner life in relation to their choices, and tend to delve deeply into past relationships and experiences.

Spiritual direction

Good spiritual direction is spiritual discernment, but is usually on a scheduled basis for about an hour, and less intensely focused on one specific issue. When faced with an especially difficult situation, a person in spiritual direction generally finds that a discernment group provides a longer, more concentrated effort plus the benefit of more people who bring additional perspective, insight, and prayer power.

Support group

Some support groups gather on a regular basis to provide encouragement and counsel to a given person. Many support groups are made up of a number of people who share a common situation (parents of young children, adults with aging parents, prostate cancer patients). Such groups meet on a regular basis to encourage one another and discuss the ways they deal with the issues that accompany their circumstances. In some cases, the group is led by a person with expertise in the field that brings them together.

A Prayer of Thomas Merton

God, we have no idea where we are going. We do not see the road ahead of us. We cannot know for certain where it will end. Nor do we really know ourselves, and the fact that we think we are following your will does not mean that we are actually doing so. But we believe that the desire to please you does in fact please you. And we hope we have that desire in all that we are doing. We hope that we will never do anything apart from that desire. And we know that if we do this you will lead us by the right road, though we may know nothing about it. Therefore, we will trust you always though we may seem to be lost and in the shadow of death. We will not fear, for you are ever with us, and you will never leave us to face our perils alone.

Thoughts in Solitude, p. 83, adapted

heartlinks

an interactive meditation website from Listening Hearts Ministries

The stillness and sacred space of a Listening Hearts program is accessible to anyone, any day of the year. Join with those seeking openness to God's call by visiting the meditation website *Heartlinks* at *http://blog.listeninghearts.org.*

Heartlinks offers visitors spiritual refreshment through structured meditations and the opportunity to share their reflections with one another. Each meditation features a Scriptural passage along with a creative, contemplative activity.

The meditation library includes:
Create a Symbol

Meditation with a Stone

Mold Clay

Take a Walk

Water Painting

Write a Hymn

A Meditative Collage

Join the growing community of people bringing the practice of spiritual discernment into their living rooms, offices, and backyards. These simple meditations will nurture your spirit, wherever you may be in your journey. Nourish your spiritual life, bring clarity and renewed energy to your days, and deepen your relationship with God. Visit *http://blog.listeninghearts.org.*